WITHOUT CONSENT
A Comprehensive Study of Missing Time
and Abduction Phenomena in the United Kingdom

Carl Nagaitis and Philip Mantle

Ringpull

First published by Ringpull Press Limited 1994

Ringpull Press Limited
Queensway House
London Road South
Poynton
Cheshire
SK12 1NJ

ISBN 1898051 08 9

A CIP catalogue record for this book is available from the British Library

Typeset by Datix International Ltd, Bungay, Suffolk
Printed in England by Clays Ltd, St Ives plc

Carl Nagaitis is a freelance journalist and writer.

Philip Mantle is the Director of Investigations for the British UFO Research Association (BUFORA), is the Mutual UFO Network's (MUFON) representative for England, and is an honorary member of the Research Institute on Anomalous Phenomenon (RIAP) in the Ukraine.

ACKNOWLEDGEMENTS

In writing a book such as this, it is inevitable that the authors will make use of research conducted by individual UFO investigators and various UFO research groups throughout the United Kingdom and overseas. With this in mind, we would sincerely like to give credit to the following individuals and UFO research groups.

First and foremost, our long-suffering partners Susan Mantle and Helen Keymer. Without their patience and indulgence, this book would not have been possible.

UFO investigators and researchers:

Ken Phillips, Albert Budden, Andy Roberts, Jenny Randles, Peter Hough, Malcolm Robinson, Steven Gamble, Michael Soper, Dr John Shaw, John Spencer, Clive Potter, David Atkins, David Kelly, Margaret Fry, Geoffrey Ambler, Andy Collins, Barry King, Tony Dodd, Graham Birdsall, Harry Harris, David Taylor, Janet Bord, Kevin Flannery, Margaret Westwood, Gloria Dixon, Paul Allison, David Haisell and any others we have forgotten to mention.

UFO research groups:

British UFO Research Association (BUFORA), Independent UFO Network (IUN), Contact UK, UFO Investigators Network (UFOIN), UFO Studies Information Services (UFOIS), Midlands UFO Network, Mutual UFO Network (MUFON), J. Allen Hynek Center for UFO Studies (CUFOS), Manchester UFO Research Association (MUFORA), Strange Phenomena Investigations (SPI), Project Hassdalen-UFO Norway/UFO Sweden.

Last but not least, the authors wish to express their gratitude to all of the individual witnesses who have been interviewed for inclusion in this book. Without their willingness to come forward this book would not exist. At times they have shown great strength and courage, and despite scorn and ridicule they have remained steadfast in their convictions. It is hoped that they will be an example to all other witnesses who have yet to find the courage to come forward and help find an answer to this most enigmatic of puzzles; the abduction phenomenon.

WITHOUT CONSENT
Carl Nagaitis & Philip Mantle

CONTENTS

ABDUCTION: THE ENIGMA

ABDUCTION: To carry off secretly. To draw away. To remove without consent. The dictionary definitions are chilling enough. The simple word often brings back memories of the sort of unpleasant events that, sadly, we have become used to reading in our newspapers: child abductions, abductions by terrorists, the abductions perpetrated by kidnappers, whether for political or financial gain. The very word is quite enough to strike fear into the hearts of most ordinary folk.

Yet today that very same word has a somewhat different meaning. Most will not know that it has come to describe another frightening phenomenon that a growing number of people are experiencing . . . alleged alien abduction.

Alien abduction is the temporary taking of a person, or persons, by beings from beyond this world. Victims, and there are many, often tell of being mysteriously transported to strange and unfamiliar places, perhaps spacecraft, where they undergo some form of examination, presumed to be medical in nature. Some victims, or to use the more correct term, abductees, are able to describe these events in great detail while others seem to bury their experiences in the depths of their minds, and that detail may only be accessible through hypnosis.

The majority of abductees are often only aware of experiencing *missing time*. They might find themselves arriving home much later than they anticipated; their last recollection being leaving work and with absolutely no idea of where they were or what they were doing in the intervening time. Some might seem to vanish off the face of the earth for short periods during their waking hours without a hint of a memory about those missing minutes or hours.

Others report possible nocturnal abductions – too real to be nightmares – in the form of visitations by alien beings or encounters with fantastic spacecraft. When amnesia locks away these experiences, hypnotic regression can provide the key which will admit the determined investigator to a treasure trove of abduction memories.

But what is the truth behind this bizarre affliction of the late twentieth century? Fact or fiction, a final frontier or a flight of fantasy?

Bizarre it is. But the twentieth century cannot claim exclusive rights to the abduction mystery. It has been around for thousands of years. Gods and goblins, phantoms and fairies – they've all been blamed for the abductions that can be found scattered through ancient mythology and less ancient fairy tales.

So when did they become *alien* abductions?

On 24 June 1947 American pilot Kenneth Arnold first coined the term Flying Saucers to describe a group of nine UFOs he saw flying over Mount Rainier, Washington. He said they had 'skimmed' over the horizon like saucers over water.

That was the real start of Ufology – the study and research of Unidentified Flying Objects.

By the early sixties there was widespread interest in the phenomenon and the number of Ufologists – the men and women who study the subject – had grown rapidly, especially in America.

The possible link between abduction and UFOs came when Betty and Barney Hill, a young American couple, reported a UFO sighting and a period of missing time during a long car journey from Canada to their home in New Hampshire.

The Hill's incident took place in 1961 after which both Betty and Barney suffered dreadful nightmares. They sought medical help and were introduced to a psychiatrist who decided to use hypnotic regression to discover what was disturbing them.

Under hypnosis Betty and Barney told an incredible story of being abducted by aliens which astonished both them and their doctor. They described their encounter in graphic detail: a meeting with aliens, a tour of a spaceship and a medical examination.

Although reluctant, the psychiatrist allowed the couple to release their story in 1964. He wasn't convinced that their perception of events was accurate yet Betty and Barney were determined to go public.

When they did they found their experience was not unique. At about the same time an Italian and a South American were also claiming to be alien abduction victims. And if their reports were to be believed, their abductions were even earlier than the Hill case.

The mystery abductions of the past were now alien abductions ... suddenly they became a twentieth century phenomenon.

And they are being reported in ever increasing numbers to this day.

The Establishment view? Alien abduction phenomena have been consigned to the trash can of twilight-world twaddle along with ghosts, ghouls and fairies at the bottom of the garden. The fact that the flying saucer fraternity is involved only serves to further undermine its credibility as far as the cynics are concerned.

However Ufologists are well used to that sort of reaction. In response they have amassed an impressive array of statistics to support their case for research into abductions, which they regard as one small, but significant, aspect of Ufology.

Since 1947 when *flying saucer* entered the English language, a staggering FORTY MILLION UFO sightings have been logged. More than thirty UFO crash landings have been reported and abduction reports run into an astonishing TENS OF THOUSANDS.

What on earth is going on out there? Well some people, Ufologists and others, are trying to find out.

The vast majority of abduction reports come from America, where Ufology is something of a growth industry. In fact one observer recently calculated that some statistics suggest that as many as ONE IN TEN Americans have had some sort of encounter with a UFO and a significant minority of those claim abduction experiences.

The phenomenon is known throughout the rest of the world from Rio to Rotterdam, from Moscow to Memphis. Individuals report alleged abductions from the frozen wastes of northern Scandinavia to the humid hot-spots of the Amazon Basin.

So what exactly do we mean by *alien abduction*? What series of events does an individual have to experience before we can call him the victim of an alleged alien abduction?

The variety of scenarios is virtually endless, but from exhaustive study of many hundreds of abduction reports from around the world Ufologists now accept that each abductee goes through a distinct series of stages.

The 'classic' abduction, and there are some, goes something like this:

The witness, or witnesses – the Ufology term for anybody experiencing an encounter with an Unidentified Flying Object or its occupants – finds himself in either an isolated or lonely place or in a normally busy but now deserted location and sights a UFO. The sighting may be preceded by a noise, often a humming, or strange lights or both.

If the witness is in a vehicle he may experience malfunctioning of the engine and electrical systems. Around this point he will either see signs of alien activity and/or encounter an alien who may then 'escort' him into the craft. The escort may use encouragement, telepathic prompting or even a degree of force to get the witness into the craft.

Some witnesses recall being transported into the craft by means which are beyond their understanding and then encountering aliens inside the UFO.

The next stage involves examination of the witness, often some form of medical examination during which strange or apparently advanced implements or pieces of equipment are used. The examination is followed by some form of communication with the aliens. Interestingly a large proportion of abductees claim that communication is non-verbal but telepathic in nature.

A tour around the craft then often follows with some abductees claiming visits to control rooms or engine rooms. More rarely a trip around 'another world' or a strange environment may be undertaken.

Further communication between the witness and his abductors may involve questioning or warnings about the future, and promises of a return visit. The witness then leaves the craft, or loses consciousness, and finds himself back where his adventure began or may even watch the craft take off into the beyond.

By no means do all abductees experience all of the above events, but all abductees experience at least one or more of them.

After returning to their own environment abductees may experience complete or partial amnesia which manifests itself as missing time.

Abduction amnesia varies dramatically. Rarely do witnesses recall all of their experience without some form of assistance, say hypnosis. Some may have forgotten everything and be aware only of a time loss. If they are curious enough, they can seek the help of a hypnotist who can regress their mind to the point at which their recall ends and so allow them to 're-live' events once more. The value of this approach and the inherent dangers will be debated later.

Other witnesses, with absolutely no recollection of the abduction, may suffer from disturbing dreams containing aspects of their experience. As in the Hill case, the recurrent nightmares may lead them to take medical advice to get to the bottom of the problem. If their doctor suggests hypnosis then both they and their doctor are likely to be in for a surprise.

A number of those whose memories of abduction are wiped out by total amnesia can develop flash-backs, or mental images of strange occurrences. These, combined with further images from the graphic dreams which can follow an encounter, can fall into place like a jigsaw puzzle, with or without hypnosis.

So you don't have to have seen a UFO or an alien to be a possible abductee. In fact the most chilling aspect of this enigma is that if you have been snatched, for whatever reason, by beings from wherever, the chances are you would not know about it.

Theoretically there is no limit to how many of us have been taken without consent.

A US magazine recently caused a mild panic when one of their 'experts' took the above argument to extremes. Readers were told that if they could find any marks or scars on their body which they could not account for, then they were potential abductees. The publication was inundated with calls from anxious possible abductees.

Here in Britain the credibility of that theory was quickly demolished by the knobbly knee test. Delegates to a British UFO conference were asked to roll up their left trouser leg and hold up their hands if they could find a mark or scar for which they could not account. The response: 100 per cent.

The point is that there is no room for wild claims and any sort of sweeping generalisation if modern Ufology is ever going to be taken seriously.

So, what are we to make of abduction phenomenon? Is it merely a part of UFO culture or is it a phenomenon in its own right? In view of the fact that many of the abductees you will read about in this book had no involvement with Ufology until they began looking for reasons for their experiences and, since it is Ufologists who have gathered the majority of available data on the subject, we have no option but to regard abduction and alien abduction as one and the same.

Furthermore, serious Ufologists contend, and we agree, that the phenomenon is a fact. There are just too many cases involving sane, sober, decent, honest and above all very ordinary people for it to be discounted out of hand.

Whether the cause, or causes, of their experiences come from Outer Space or Inner Space, is a matter for research and further debate. But the plain fact is that a growing number of people believe they have been taken away from their familiar surroundings, albeit temporarily, and introduced to something so strange, so odd that it often changes their outlook on life completely.

Those who don't write-off their experiences as a bad dream or a bout of temporary insanity sometimes grasp the alien abduction theory with both hands because, at the very least, it offers them an explanation for the apparently inexplicable.

As we mentioned earlier, abductions didn't suddenly begin to coincide with the arrival of the term *flying saucer* back in 1947. People have been reporting mysterious abductions for centuries.

Back then the abductors were described as fairies or witches, even Gods, some of whom liked to have their wicked way with the odd lesser mortal. The UFOs were variously described as magic carpets, flying castles and even as the Chariots of the Gods we all know from author Erich von Daniken.

Stories of heroes being transported to the heavens, where they see myriad things magical and wondrous, abound in

ancient literature. Folklore and fairy tales are full of references to children being taken off by the fairies.

Celebrated American astronomer Carl Sagan dug up the
following folk tale from 1645, which illustrates the point:

'A Cornish teenager, Anne Jeffries, was found groggy and
crumpled on the floor. Much later she recalled being attacked
by little men, carried paralysed to a castle in the air, seduced
and returned home. She called the little men faeries. The
next year she was arrested for witchcraft . . .'

It is fair to speculate that a Middle Ages man confronted by
a UFO would be stumped to find the words to describe it. A
flying machine would have been a ludicrous concept in those
days so why not call it a flying castle? Some of the descriptions of aliens, allegedly encountered by some of the abductees we study in our book, make them sound not unlike the
story book perceptions of goblins, or even elves. And by the
time our Middle Age story had been passed around the
community, by word of mouth of course, it would certainly
have been decorated with the usual embellishments these
stories accumulate in the telling.

But alleged abductions of long ago are beyond investigation. No matter how easy it is to draw comparisons between
modern day abductions and those in mythology and folklore,
the latter remain no more than mythology and folklore.

Modern day abductions are fair game for thorough investigation. And thanks to 1990s communications' technology
today's abductees can, and sometimes do, find their reports
flashed around the globe almost instantly.

Modern man can no longer blame fairies and goblins for
those events and occurrences which his science is unable to
explain. So UFOs can come in handy.

Ufologists have come up with a whole host of theories to
try to explain both visitations and abductions. They range
from the physical to the psychological and even to the down-
right hysterical. Many Ufologists are less interested in UFOs
and abductions than they are in the reasons people report
these things. Some privately admit that they believe there is
little chance that the phenomenon is due to extra-terrestrials
visiting our planet. However they are prepared to keep an
open mind.

Others find the alien evidence so compelling that they are convinced extra-terrestrial activity is, indeed, the only possible explanation for the phenomenon. Within this group alone, different theories abound.

One school of thought maintains that we Earth dwellers have been visited by intelligent life forms from the depths of space since time began. They believe they have monitored us through our development and have even nudged us in the right direction at the right time. This view of a philanthropic group of aliens who have taken on the role of guardians of our planet is appealing to some. Indeed clues to support this theory can be found among the British cases which we have put under the microscope in this book.

Although modern science accepts the likelihood that there is other life among the billions of stars in our universe, why would those life forms, assuming they have the ability, travel huge distances to oversee the inhabitants of an insignificant little planet like ours?

What's in it for them? Those questions remain unanswered.

Another school of thought postulates the notion that our alien visitors come here for very selfish reasons. This school puts forward the theory that the extra-terrestrials behind UFO sightings and abductions are here to harvest a rich source of genetic material to enable them to continue their own race.

New York artist and world-renowned Ufologist Budd Hopkins has put forward this view most forcibly in recent years. Whether the alleged aliens have found themselves down a genetic cul-de-sac forcing them to look elsewhere for the means to continue reproduction is, quite frankly, anybody's guess. But Hopkins and others point to various aspects of abduction phenomena which seem to support this genetic motive.

Many abductees report a high degree of interest in their sexual and reproductive organs during on-board medical examinations. Some even claim to have had sexual relations with the visitors.

Add to that claims that human ova have been removed from some abductees and reports from others of mysteriously abandoned pregnancies coinciding with abductions – implying the removal of tiny foetuses in the most mysterious circumstances - and it all adds up to the one of the most sinister scenarios imaginable.

Some of the British abductees you will read about later in this book add further fuel to the raging debate on the sexual/human reproduction aspect of abduction.

This most disturbing of theories ties in with a spate of alleged mutilations of farm animals in the USA in recent years. Horses and cattle had whole sections of their reproductive systems removed with surgical precision, according to some reports.

The 'operations', it was claimed, had been conducted using some sort of laser instrument which had a cauterising effect on the animal tissue, researchers stated.

Intriguing, but because UFO research is undertaken largely by amateurs, some good, some not so good, gathering evidence to examine cases like these is extremely difficult. These are the sort of theories that we all know Ufologists will never prove, not unless they can first prove the existence of alien visitors piloting UFOs.

Thankfully in Britain and America we are lucky enough to have some well-respected and experienced UFO investigators who are concerned with fact and not fiction.

And whether they are dealing with UFO sightings or alleged alien abduction phenomena they are more likely to reject a case than put it up for serious consideration if it does not stand up to the test of a rigorous investigation.

Many alleged alien abduction cases are discounted because of 'contamination'. No, they are not infected with some dreadful alien disease. The term simply means that their abduction experience could have been contaminated by the mass of readily available information, in the form of literature, films and TV programmes about other people's abduction cases.

Any abductee would be hard pressed to describe the variety of new sights, sounds and sensations he experiences during his encounter.

So if that abductee is familiar with, say Whitley Streiber's *Communion*, for example, or with any of the many books and the growing number of movies on the subject of abduction, he is likely to lapse into a relevant terminology.

If he describes the classic Streiber alien – slight, almond-eyed, pinched nose, grey complexion – how can we know whether this is a description of what he has seen or what he thinks he has seen?

Is the sleek metallic craft he describes an account of a real experience or an imagined one based on a UFO picture or a description picked up from a book or the TV screen? No matter how bona fide the abductee, no matter how graphic his description of events, the serious investigator must decide whether the evidence, the physical signs and any other factors, sufficiently compensate for the level of contamination.

As with UFO sightings, the number of people reporting abduction phenomena is far greater in the United States than in the UK. This is not just because the population of America is far greater. It has more to do with the character of the nation.

A relatively new country, America is still more prepared to take on the unusual, to welcome the new and to be more open-minded about strange concepts and ideas. After all, as we have already pointed out, it was an American who first used the term 'flying saucer'.

Flying saucer witnesses in America are more likely to speak openly about their experiences than in stiff upper-lipped Britain. Americans have a ready-made audience, eager to hear the tiniest details from the scores of UFO magazines published all over the country.

To the population of the nation which, for many years, led the space race, spaceships are a reality. Maybe flying saucers are just the next step.

In fact some of the heroic astronauts from the National Aeronautics and Space Administration (NASA) have given a personal boost to the cause of Ufology.

One of the most interesting reports came from Gemini 4 astronaut James McDivitt, in June 1965. Orbiting 90 miles above the earth he saw a cylinder-shaped object, with arms protruding from it, in apparent free flight over the Pacific Ocean.

Travelling at a higher altitude, the object moved along a parallel path to the Gemini, but seemed to be closing fast. McDivitt and fellow astronaut Edward White were preparing to take evasive action when the object disappeared.

McDivitt had taken a photo and some cine film of the object. The official version was that he had spotted the unmanned satellite Pegasus. But on checking, McDivitt discovered that it would have been twelve hundred miles away from his position when he sighted it.

Captain Ed Mitchell, the sixth man to walk on the moon, said in 1974: 'I am completely convinced that some UFO sightings are real. The question is not where the UFOs are from. The question is what they are.'

These are just two of an estimated thirty UFO sightings by astronauts. They became so common NASA came up with a codeword for them 'Bogeys'.

These well-publicised incidents and comments have given American Ufologists a credibility that can only be envied on this side of the Atlantic.

Like UFO spotters, American abductees have come forward in their thousands to tell their stories or write their books.

This has got much to do with the power of the mighty dollar. We remarked earlier on the way Ufology in the States has become something of a growth industry, and a good abduction case can mean that some abductees can cash in on the wider public interest. Lucrative book and film deals and radio and TV appearances offer celebrity status, albeit temporary, to many abductees and UFO witnesses in the States.

And if there is one thing Americans love dearly it is a celebrity.

Hollywood's most recent abduction success story, in movie terms, was *Fire In the Sky*, which was a box office hit when it was released in 1993.

It followed the story of American logger Travis Walton who became an abduction victim in 1975. While his mystery vanishing act sparked a major police hunt, Walton was going through the classic stages of alien abduction. Police interviewed his workmates — worried that Walton's disappearance could have been the result of foul play — but the bemused logger turned up just in time to prevent any miscarriage of justice and with a story that was literally out of this world.

Walton went on to write a bestseller about his abduction and when senior members of the Hollywood industry met with the humble logger to discuss the film project they said they had been impressed by his sincerity. After that meeting, they had no hesitation in turning his account into a big screen production.

When he came to Britain to publicise his film, Walton said he had found people in his own country anxious to hear his story and he was grateful for the assistance he had received from UFO investigators. He never once complained of the cynical reception that many British abductees say they receive in this country.

Ironically the openness of the American approach to both UFOs and Abduction Phenomenon makes the reaction of British scoffers even more pronounced.

'Only the Americans would fall for that nonsense,' is the usual response when discussing the subject here. Any attempt at a serious discussion on Ufology or alien abduction phenomenon is received with raised eyebrows and wry smiles.

With attitudes such as this it is hard to blame British abductees for keeping their heads below the parapet. It probably explains why we have only forty catalogued cases in this country, when UFO investigators are convinced there are many, many more who are unwilling to admit their experiences, let alone talk about them. As one victim said recently: 'For me, becoming an abductee was like contracting a socially embarrassing disease.'

Why? Because he let it be known that he believed his abductors were not of this world. An intelligent and articulate man, he has carefully considered who or what were responsible for a bizarre series of events he experienced some years ago and he has come to the sober conclusion that he was abducted by aliens who travelled to this Earth in a spacecraft.

He has no idea why they took him or why they examined him or from where they came.

He has eliminated all other rational explanations for his

experience and settled for the only theory that seems to add up.

To the handful of people he confided in over the years, his story represents the rantings of a wacky weirdo, a member of the lunatic fringe with flying saucers on the brain. He quickly learned that silence was his best protection.

Today, he is Mr Normal, Mr Respectable, pursuing a safe and sensible career. He denies any knowledge of abduction phenomenon except on the very rare occasions when he meets a fellow abductee. Even then he is reluctant to open up on the subject until he is assured that he has got a sympathetic ear.

However, the British reserve is not totally negative as far as Ufologists are concerned. The fact that alleged abductees risk having ridicule heaped upon them when they talk publicly about their experiences *must* deter the cranks and the attention seekers.

The fact that some are willing to come out and talk about their abductions indicates a determination to get to the bottom of a phenomenon which has had an impact on their lives. They are prepared to risk the ridicule in the interests of research.

British abductees have much to lose and little to gain by going public. Unlike their American brothers and sisters they will not become temporary celebrities and they don't stand to get a fat cheque from a Hollywood producer.

For the purposes of this book we have persuaded abductees from across the country to tell their stories in the first ever catalogue of British abduction cases. Some have allowed us to use their real names, others have chosen to use pseudonyms for obvious reasons.

Some are coming forward for the first time and others have been prepared to reveal aspects of their cases that they have never spoken about before.

Each and every one of the following cases has been investigated and researched by investigators of the British UFO Research Association, individual independent UFO investigators, and other UFO research groups within the UK.

We have reconstructed events as related to us in detail by the abductees or from the hundreds of pages of data from the files of BUFORA. Transcripts of scores of taped interviews and hypnosis sessions have been checked and cross-checked to give the most accurate account possible.

Each of our abductees has their own theory about abduction phenomena, aliens and UFOs and those terms are used freely in their accounts. They have also been invited to give their own explanation of what they feel they went through.

We know how frustrating it can be to read of strange phenomena where the only cases available to illustrate events come from thousands of miles away. The stories of abduction from the United States and elsewhere in the world are legion but their remoteness means we sometimes have difficulty getting a grip on the subject.

In this book we present British cases involving ordinary people who find themselves caught up in extraordinary circumstances. These are real people and to them their stories are equally real.

We take a neutral stance.

Abduction phenomenon is fact. Alien abduction? We leave you to decide.

CEIVs

Alien abductions cases are known as Close Encounters of the Fourth Kind (CEIVs). Encounters of the First Kind (CEIs) are basically UFO sightings, but at relatively close range. Encounters of the Second Kind (CEIIs) are incidents where the UFO leaves some kind of mark on the environment, burn marks on the ground or any area of flattened vegetation to indicate the landing area of a vehicle.

Close Encounters of the Third Kind (CEIIIs) are understood by most people thanks to the Hollywood blockbuster of the same name. These events are sightings of UFOs where an occupant or alien being is involved.

Fourth Kind encounters are the least common of UFO events, often the most dramatic and invariably the most difficult to investigate. They centre on the abduction of the witness or witnesses. The credibility of those witnesses is therefore crucial to establishing exactly what happened to them.

The UFO investigator, faced with an alleged abduction, will first scrutinise the abductee. Is he or she sane, free from drink or drug problems, of a stable background? The investigator has to make sure that the trip experienced was not drink or drug induced and was not the result of a sick mind.

He will also need to check out the abductee's general state of health because if he or she were taking any medication, for whatever complaint, he will need to ascertain whether the drugs prescribed could have any side effects, like hallucination.

The general physical and mental check is a means of clearing the ground for the next stage of the investigation. Is the witness free from personal emotional crises? Sadly there are some people who concoct stories to draw attention to themselves. Often they are the victims of personal problems and the creation of a fantasy scenario is their cry for help. They may just crave attention: want somebody to pay attention to them and spend some time with them. If that means fabricating a story so be it.

Is the witness a publicity seeker, motivated by seeing their name in print? Is he or she out to make a fast pound? Some people, for whatever reason, will create an encounter not for personal attention, but public attention. The celebrity status they enjoy from local publicity is minimal, yet for some it is motive enough. Others mistakenly believe they can sell their UFO or abduction accounts to newspapers.

All these possibilities will go through the investigator's mind before he can begin the investigation proper.

The real work starts with the interview. The investigator spends a great deal of time in personal interviews with witnesses. An investigation will take a witness through their experiences step by step, often probing for the sort of detail that the interviewee might regard as insignificant.

Throughout this process, the interviewer will be paying great attention to the witness's body language, tone of voice and mannerisms. These can reveal much about the character of the witness. Sitting chatting in the home environment of the witness can provide useful background on the type of person making the claims.

So when the physical clues are sadly lacking, when the evidence, as is often the case, is very thin on the ground, the investigator can weigh-up the facts and make a balanced judgement on the case.

As one experienced investigator explained: 'After spending a great deal of time with a witness you can get a gut reaction. You may just know he is, or sometimes isn't, telling the truth.'

When the investigator has completed his interviews, nearly always witnessed and tape recorded, he will then go through the witness statement with a fine-tooth comb.

Did the UFO leave any physical mark on the environment in any way? Did the alleged occupants leave any kind of physical mark upon the witness? Did the witness have the opportunity to make any recordings or take any pictures of who or what he had seen? Although we don't know of any cases of witnesses being armed with tape recorders and cameras one of those abductees who recounts his story in the following pages did indeed manage to take a snap of an alleged alien visitor.

Proving any abduction case is well nigh impossible at the present time. As BUFORA knows only too well, providing conclusive evidence of a Close Encounter of the Fourth Kind would also involve finding conclusive proof of the existence of UFOs and aliens . . . and nobody has managed to do that quite yet.

However an investigator can put forward a case for serious consideration if the witness or abductee is of sufficient quality. If they are decent, sound of mind individuals and if it can be demonstrated that they have nothing to gain, and in some cases much to lose by talking about their experiences, then they become candidates for our catalogue of study.

The two cases we will now highlight are not untypical of many abduction reports. They all rely heavily on the testimony of the witnesses.

All three alleged abductees were alone when they experienced their encounters and there was no physical evidence to support their claims. In one of the cases there were no corroborating reports of sightings or events to support their perceptions.

However investigators were impressed by the sincerity of all, none of whom sought publicity.

All of these abductees stood to gain nothing by telling their stories and two of them suffered disturbing after-effects in the form of nightmares in the months following their encounters.

Elsie Oakensen,
22 November 1978,
Church Stowe,
Northamptonshire.

Elsie Oakensen, head of the Daventry Teacher Training Centre, pulled her coat around her as she left her office at about 5.15 p.m. It was a chill winter's evening, the fifty year old working wife and mother felt the North East wind sting her face as she stopped to buy a newspaper before making her way to her car.

She noticed that a side-light on her vehicle was not working, so she decided to make the seven mile journey home driving with dipped headlights. A sensible woman, Mrs Oakensen was not one to take chances in the fast fading light. She had made the trip between her office and her home in the village of Church Stowe near Weedon so many times that she was familiar with every turn in the road. But the wife of a police Chief Inspector knew better than to take chances when it came to road safety.

It was an uneventful journey until she joined the busy A5 just two miles from her home village. As she manoeuvred her car onto the fast dual carriageway, she became aware of a sight she would never forget.

Ahead of her, about one hundred feet above the smooth tarmac surface of the A5, was an object so strange, so unnatural that she had to struggle to find words to describe it.

A dumbbell-shaped object, grey and plastic looking, with a brilliant red light in the left hand sphere and a green light in the right hand sphere just ... well it just hovered there. It didn't move. It simply floated. From the way it spanned the entire width of the dual carriageway Elsie guess-timated this strange something to be at least fifty feet in length.

'I was absolutely fascinated by it,' Elsie told us some time later. 'But I just drove on as normal.'

Gripped by a combination of both curiosity and awe, Elsie resolutely gripped the steering wheel and drove on, directly towards and then under the bizarre object.

'I had to drive on so I could take my usual right turn off the A5 at Stowe Hill,' she said.

'I remember at first thinking that it must be some kind of aeroplane and that it would zoom over my head and crash behind me. But it just hung in the air,' recalled Elsie.

'I remember, once I had turned off the A5, looking back and thinking it must have gone by now, but it hadn't. It was still there, those brilliant lights still shining.'

The encounter had been so absorbing that Elsie could not recall seeing any other traffic on that section of the A5. But it would have been highly unusual for that busy section of road to be deserted at that time, when many people were returning home from work.

The darkness continued to close around Elsie's car as she proceeded with the final leg of her journey home. 'How strange,' she thought to herself. 'What could that have been all about?'

She made her way along the narrow, winding country road, taking a right turn at a T-junction on the outskirts of Church Stowe. Completing the turn she changed up to third gear. Oddly the car seemed to slow down instead of speed up.

Momentarily forgetting the mysterious object over the A5, she double checked she had the accelerator fully depressed and then in desperation changed down to first in a desperate bid to start the car moving.

At last the engine seemed to respond, but when she came to the end of a line of trees by the entrance to a farm at the perimeter of the village, the motor just cut-out.

Elsie found herself sitting in complete darkness, and complete silence. The engine had stopped and every light on the vehicle had been extinguished. Turning the ignition key was useless, the car was dead.

Elsie looked out of the car windows into total blackness. Putting her face close to the glass, so she could peer out, she thought she would catch a glimpse of the lights from the houses and farm buildings nearby. But there was nothing. She could not even make out the shapes of any of the familiar buildings she drove by every day.

'I don't know why, but I wasn't frightened,' she said. 'But

that was before the events became even stranger than at first.'

Suddenly a brilliant circle of pure white light appeared and illuminated the road by the passenger side of the car.

'Then as suddenly as it came on, it went off and I was in darkness once again,' recalled Elsie.

Seconds later further circles of light, about a meter across, appeared first at the front of the car, then at the rear and then at each side. Punctuating the pitch darkness, they flicked on, then off, then on again.

At one moment Elsie thought the glow from one of the circles illuminated the farm entrance, at another all she could see beyond the strange light was blackness.

Punching holes in the night, the circles of light danced around her car in an almost choreographed routine as if searching for something . . . .or someone.

'Yes, they were searching,' said Elsie. 'They seemed to be searching the darkness. I would have called them search-lights, but I remember realising they couldn't have been caused by a searchlight because there was no beam.'

Suddenly Elsie found herself thirty yards further down the road, the motor was running, the car was in third gear and she was behind the wheel and driving quite normally.

Her head was whirling. Moments ago, Elsie was stranded in a broken-down car, surrounded by darkness. Now she was back in control and driving home. But she had no idea of what had occurred in the intervening seconds.

As if to reassure herself, she looked around and could see the shapes of the local church and other buildings silhouetted against the evening skyline. 'Yes, I'm nearly home now,' she said to herself. 'Not far now.'

As she parked up outside her home, Elsie noticed her broken sidelight was now working again. She glanced at her house and could see her kitchen lights were on. Good, that meant husband John was home and would be preparing the evening meal.

He had been working split-shifts so it was quite normal for him to prepare the tea while waiting for his wife to return home from work.

Elsie put the car in the garage and let herself into the

house. It was then that she glanced down at her watch. She was stunned. Somehow her fifteen minute journey home had taken half an hour, twice as long as normal, although her car had seemed stationary for mere moments.

'I told John, "I will just go upstairs to look out of the window and then I will tell you something you won't believe".'

From the bedroom window Elsie saw a flashing yellow light in the same position in which she had seen the dumbbell-shaped object.

'I went down and told John exactly what had happened,' said Elsie later. 'He didn't say a word. He just dished out the meal. When I told him my story I didn't mention the word UFO. I don't think I had ever heard that word.'

At exactly 7 p.m. that evening Elsie felt a tightening sensation around her head. The band of pressure stretched across her forehead and around to the back of her cranium. The strange restrictive sensation, like having a powerful elastic band placed around one's head, lasted about a minute and then disappeared completely. She suddenly recalled experiencing the same sensation at lunchtime that day.

That would have been the end of Elsie Oakensen's intriguing experience if it hadn't been for a young man at her office.

Back at the Daventry Teacher Training Centre next day the youngster overheard Elsie relating her experience to colleagues during a break for coffee.

'Sounds like a UFO to me', he said suddenly, causing Elsie to sit up, a perplexed expression on her face.

'An Unidentified Flying Object, you know flying saucers,' added the young man before launching into a brief explanation of the phenomenon for the benefit of an audience comprising of Elsie and a handful of fellow office workers.

Elsie's bizarre experience was about to become a Close Encounter of the office gossip kind.

Her missing time mystery was light years away from the usual tittle-tattle that broke up the humdrum routine of office life. The story soon spread beyond the confines of the training centre and before long a reporter from the Northampton Chronicle and Echo turned up to interview Elsie.

Devoting twelve column inches to her sighting, the article in the Friday 24th November edition of the paper reported several more incidents in and around the area that week. A woman in Northampton claimed to have seen a 'window in the sky' with green flashing lights around it. But there was no mention of the strange dumbbell-shaped object with a green light in one end and a red one in the other.

British UFO Research Association investigators were soon on the case and took detailed notes of the Oakensen case. Elsie, by now, was anxious to learn as much about what happened to her as possible and was more than happy to co-operate.

With the investigation almost complete there was only one further course open to them. Would Mrs Oakensen agree to hypnosis?

When she said 'of course' the BUFORA team were delighted. They explained that hypnotic regression was a method which could take Elsie's mind back to that fateful evening enabling her to 're-live' the events, particularly during the period of her time loss.

A qualified hypnotherapist put Elsie into a hypnotic trance and led her mind back to those anxious moments in her car. During the hypnosis session, which took place in August 1979, nine months after her encounter, a detailed record of her recollections, and of her reactions were taken.

Elsie said: 'My car engine has stalled, I feel hot. A band tightens around my head as it did at lunch time. I am getting hotter and beginning to sweat. The pressure hurts . . . it hurts my head.

'A brilliant white light is shining in my eyes, a pure white light, very bright. Circles of very bright light radiate from it as it comes closer until I can only see the top of the circles . . . my body gets hotter . . . the pain in my head is intense.

'I feel as if I am sitting. I can't feel my legs. My arms are shaking. I am very frightened. The radiating circles of light seem to change to a small brilliant circle, obviously going away from me.

'It's still light, but hazy and through this haze materialise two shapes. The first is a long, thin shape that appears to the left and then disappears. The second is more rectangular and appears to the right – disappears – then both appear together. They shine through the haze, a silver glow outlines both grey-coloured shapes which are smooth and rounded, rather ghostlike. The bright light now shines as a small circle in the distance. I get hotter, my arms shake more, my head hurts dreadfully. I am terrified.'

At that stage Elsie's discomfort and distress was such that she was immediately taken out of the trance by the hypno-therapist. The investigators were disappointed that the regression had not revealed more clear detail of Elsie's encounter.

But the lack of any more vivid descriptions did not rule out the possibility of it being consistent with alien abduction.

The sighting of the UFO, the lights, the malfunctioning of her car and the missing time certainly make the episode a contender for Fourth Kind encounter status.

Was Elsie and her car taken up into a UFO? It has happened to some American abductees, if their reports are to be believed. Without filling in her missing time we'll probably never know the truth.

Investigators agree that Elsie's experience is an interesting example of alien abduction phenomenon, but not so much because the events tie in with so many other abduction reports. What makes this case worthy of attention is the quality of the witness.

She is undoubtedly a credible witness. A mature and responsible woman in a senior position in a professional career and with a husband in the police force. Elsie is no crackpot, far from it.

Contamination doesn't come into this case at all. Elsie had never even heard of UFOs and had no interest in the subject. She had not been influenced by UFO literature. She had never seen such literature and she was so ignorant of the flying saucer phenomenon that she could only liken the object she saw to an aeroplane.

Elsie's only regret about the incident was the reaction which she and her husband received from some people after she had agreed to give an interview to the reporter from the local newspaper.

Her husband John suffered some mockery from colleagues in the force and a few locals ridiculed Elsie's report. In fact on one occasion a man called at the front door of her home and when she opened it he simply stood there guffawing.

'I was furious,' said Elsie. 'What these people didn't seem to understand was that I was not making any claims about what happened to me. I didn't describe that thing over the A5 as a UFO. I simply told people, as honestly as I could, what had happened to me.

'Interestingly enough, when John retired from the force we had visits from other ex-police officers. Some of them told me how bad they felt about the way John had been treated by some. Then they went on to tell me they had seen strange things and heard reports that they dare not admit for fear of becoming victims of ridicule themselves,' added Elsie.

Although there had been no corroborative sightings of the strange UFO seen by Elsie on that November night in 1978, it later transpired that four Women's Institute members may well have seen the same object just two hours later.

The four ladies were travelling by car from Byfield via Woodford Halse towards Preston Capes – just a stone's throw from Elsie's home village of Church Stowe. They would have been passing through that area at sometime after seven that same night.

First the driver of their car saw what she later described as a parallel-sided beam of light shoot out from the clouds. Seconds later it disappeared. Then the beam appeared again, although this time only momentarily.

The direction of the beam? Ironically, it seemed to be aiming for Church Stowe.

Then as the driver turned into the Preston Capes road, she and her passengers could not help but notice a strange object in the sky. They described it as comprising of 'two lights, one red and one green' and the lights seemed to be about 12 inches apart, indicating that if it was the same dumbbell-shaped object seen by Mrs Oakensen then it must have been some considerable distance away for its new observers.

Pressing on, the driver continued along her route trying to suppress the feeling that they were being followed. One look out of the window seemed to confirm their worst fears. The object was pacing their car. For one heart-stopping moment, the engine of the vehicle faltered, threatening to cut-out as it swept along on the final leg of the journey to Preston Capes.

Top: Taken by Stephen Darbishire, February 1954 in the Lake District, England. Courtesy Fortean Picture Library. Above; Taken by James W. Allen in October 1980 over Pitlochry, Scotland. Courtesy J. Allen Hynek Centre for the UFO Studies.
Unless otherwise stated all photographs are courtesy Philip Mantle.

Top: Taken by Franklin Youri on October 8, 1978 over Tehran, Iran.
Courtesy J. Allen Hynek Centre. Above: Taken by Hannah McRoberts in
October 1981 over Vancouver, British Columbia, Canada. Courtesy J. Allen
Hynek Centre.

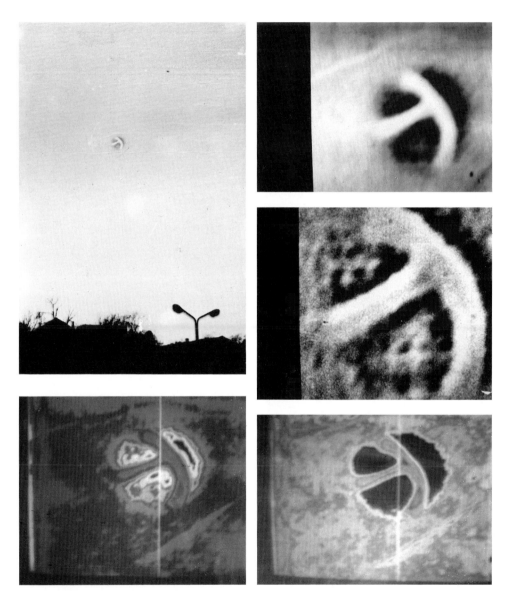

Main Photograph: 8 November, 1989 over the Town of Voronezh, Russia, Courtesy Uri E. Lozotsev. Inserts: Computer enhanced images of above. Courtesy Ground Saucer Watch.

Top: Moutunau, New Zealand. Photographed declared 'inscrutable' by two ex-Royal New Zealand Air Force Photographic section members. Above: February 19th, 1994, Craiglusker Reservoir Central Scotland. Taken by Ian Macpherson. Photo-case is still under investigation by SPI and BUFORA.
Courtesy Ian Macpherson

The driver knocked it into third gear and rammed her foot down on the accelerator. The motor responded energetically and the vehicle powered on. The lights moved off and out of sight in seconds enabling them to cover the remaining miles without interruption.

Had those ladies, as Elsie believes happened to her, also been trailed? And had the driver's quick reactions saved them from an encounter similar to that experienced by Mrs Oakensen? We will probably never find out.

Today, sixteen years on, Elsie is still searching for answers to an experience which changed her life. Now retired, the mother of three and grandmother to four, is still prepared to assist Ufologists in their work, in the hope that it might provide some answers, one day.

Privately, Elsie takes the view that her encounter was more spiritual in nature than an event caused by alien beings. This has been reinforced by the discovery that she has developed the 'gift' of healing, and has joined the National Federation of Spiritual Healers.

'It is something that came to me after my experience,' said Elsie. 'It is a gift I certainly didn't have before. Now I find that I can help others with my gift and I will certainly continue using it.

'I don't know for sure what happened to me that night. All I do know is something very definitely did occur. In a way I'm a richer person for it.'

Graham Allen,
17 June 1979,
Newbury,
Berkshire.

Painter and decorator Graham Allen was just twenty years old when he had what he is now convinced was a Close Encounter of the Fourth Kind.

Back then Graham was living in Staffordshire and his fiancée Charlotte, now his wife, was living in Maidenhead, Berkshire.

The long distance lovers had come to an arrangement to ensure that they could spend every precious weekend together. One weekend he would do the travelling and stay over at Charlotte's home, the next it would be her turn to make the trek and stay with him.

This particular weekend it was Graham's turn to travel and as luck had it he had been working in Birmingham which meant he faced a slightly shorter drive than usual.

'It was the Friday before the longest day of 1979,' recalls Graham. 'Having checked the date on the calendar that makes it June 17th. I'd been working in Birmingham, a place called Shirley, which was actually closer to Maidenhead for me because I was already on the A34, my usual route.'

He knocked off at sometime after 4 p.m. that day, put away his work things and grabbed his weekend bag. As he stepped out into the open the warmth of the afternoon hit him immediately. The sun had been beating down all day long and when he climbed into his car the interior was like a hot house.

Winding down the driver window for a bit of fresh air, he set off at about 4.30 p.m. on a route he knew well; he was looking forward to a smooth run.

Sun shining, very warm and light traffic . . . perfect conditions to drive down to spend the weekend with the woman he loved.

Driving along with the radio on and a cooling draught from the open window, Graham made good progress through Stratford-Upon-Avon despite the tourist traffic. He soon got down to the Oxford ring road, where, after negotiating lighter than normal rush-hour traffic, he motored southwards into the open countryside, his normal turning to Maidenhead fast approaching.

'I remember sitting at a traffic island, and a sports car with some girls in it shot across in front of me. I remember going around the island with the radio going and the DJ saying "and now the time is five minutes to six".'

A few minutes into the next record and the car radio began to play up. First it spluttered, then it crackled furiously and then it faded away completely.

'Must be passing under power cables,' Graham remembers thinking to himself. 'It'll clear in a minute.'

But it didn't clear. Determined not to lose the company of his radio, Graham , one hand on the steering wheel, leaned over awkwardly, fingers groping for the control knobs that would hopefully enable him to re-tune the set.

It was no use. No matter which way he turned them the radio stayed stubbornly silent. For a few short seconds he took his eyes off the road and glared at the radio as if he might spot the fault. The radio lights were on, he couldn't see any problem, but the speakers were dead.

When he looked up, gone were the blue skies and the sunshine of a few seconds ago. The sky was overcast and rain was teeming down.

Shaking his head in disbelief, he was forced to switch on his wipers to clear the huge splatters of rain that now obscured his vision through the windscreen.

'I think I assumed it was some sort of a sun shower or something. I remember thinking those girls in the sports car would get wet.

'But it was a very dramatic change, from a balmy afternoon to a grey, wet day.'

It took him a few seconds to accustom himself to the change of scene, but slightly confused he continued driving. Then gradually that confusion changed to a growing sense of unease. For some reason he didn't seem to recognise what should have been a very familiar route.

The landmarks he passed, the buildings, the churches, the cottages: none of them were ringing any bells. Yet he had travelled this route so often it was incredible that he did not see something he recognised.

As he drove his car along the dual carriageway, he scanned the horizon for any clues as to how close was his turn off.

Then suddenly, his fear was confirmed. He saw that the road sign he was approaching said 'Newbury 3 miles'.

He had missed his turning. How could he possibly have missed the road to Maidenhead? He'd never done it before; it was well-signposted and he would have seen it coming up. Furious with himself, he moved into the centre of the carriageway and turned right into the entrance to a farm.

The next thing Graham remembered was sitting in his car, the engine running, the radio working normally. The car was still in the farm entrance but now it was facing the dual carriageway.

The rain had stopped; the car and the road were completely dry.

Now Graham was really confused. There was only one thing to do, he would have to retrace his route to get back to the correct turning for Maidenhead. Glancing at the car clock, he saw it was now five past six, ten minutes since the last time-check by the DJ, and that was before his turning. He shouldn't have far to go back to his turning, he thought.

Graham was stunned when he discovered that the missed turning was fifteen miles back along the road, and the spot where he had heard the first time check was a further five miles away.

Somehow he had driven twenty miles in just ten minutes.

The rest of his journey to Maidenhead was uneventful. He arrived at 7.15 p.m. although he had been expected at 6.30 p.m.

'My fiancée was waiting for me when I got there,' recalled Graham. 'She came running out of the house. But I couldn't get out of the car. My legs were like blocks and they would not move. They were shaking. I felt sort of cold and clammy and Charlotte thought this was hilarious for some reason.

'She helped me out of the car, laughing her head off, and I just said "You're not going to believe this". I then told her the whole story over a cup of tea.'

Over the next few weeks and months, Graham's sleep was regularly interrupted by bizarre flash-backs of incidents and events which he could not place. Things that he seemed to know had happened to him, but didn't know when or where.

Mystified, he tried to put these bad dreams, as he called them, into the back of his mind, and to some extent succeeded until Christmas 1987. That was when the entire encounter of 17th June 1979 returned to haunt him.

Graham and Charlotte were now living at Rugeley, Staffordshire, with their four children. They had retired to bed that night at their normal time, but Graham was suddenly woken at 3 a.m.

'I was back in my car again on that summer day all those years ago,' said Graham. 'Suddenly it was surrounded by a golden light. The car had been stationary and I could hear a low humming all around.

'Then I saw a man with a dog on the opposite side of the road and that's when I started to panic. I shouted and called to the man to help me.'

The humming became more intense and the golden light glowed more strongly as the car, slowly but surely, began to lift from the ground.

'I could feel the car rising and then everything went black,' remembered Graham. 'Next I can feel this high-pitched noise in my head and then I find myself in a brightly-lit room, lying on a smooth surface.'

Graham was lying on his back and unable to move. He slowly opened his eyes to see three figures, alien figures, looking at him. Large eyes, smooth skinned, the beings, who Graham was unable to describe in great detail, seemed to be doing something to him.

Suddenly Graham awoke to find himself in bed. From above there was a loud humming noise, loud enough to wake his wife and children.

Graham has been interviewed by a number of Ufologists who agree his case could be a CEIV. He has provided them with drawings of the beings he saw in his dream and has been happy to co-operate with researchers, having developed a great interest in the subject.

Now committed to the alien abduction theory Graham has had some odd after-effects following his experience. He claims to have received telepathic messages of various sorts on a number of occasions, including information on the construction of anti-gravity devices.

At the time of his 1979 experience there was no indication that Graham had been contaminated by UFO or other literature. The subject was then completely new to him.

Today, his interest in Ufology is such that he liases with other UFO 'contactees' to exchange information.

David Thomas (pseudonym),
8 February 1985,
Pwllheli,
North Wales.

David Thomas knew the four and a half mile trek to his village from Pwllheli like the back of his hand. It didn't matter that it was three in the morning and black as hell, the starlight was all he needed to make his way home.

He was just grateful that the heavy snows that had fallen over much of Britain that day had missed the lovely Lleyn Peninsula. The warmth of the Irish Sea helps to temper the worst excesses of winter.

Although there was some snow on the ground and an arctic chill in the air David hardly felt it. He'd just enjoyed a hot night of music with his mates. The beat was still pounding in the head of this unemployed nineteen year old.

About twenty minutes down the road David could have sworn that the music was still playing in his ears. He stopped, shook his head and then listened.

Silence, a deafening silence. An eerie stillness devoid of the night-time noises every country boy grows up with. No rustle in the grass, no owls' wing-beat, not even a whispering wind.

Then yes, there it was. Not music but a humming. Faint, but a humming nevertheless. It was like the low-pitched thrum of an electricity generator, but David knew this part of the world well enough to be certain that there wasn't one in operation for many miles.

He peered through the darkness, across to the field where the noise seemed to be coming from. Turning his head first this way, then that way, he tried to get a bearing on the source of the sound.

It was no good. He'd have to go and see what it was. He left the road and padded over the frozen grass of the field. As he made his way over the field the only noise to break into the insistent thrumming was that made by his feet crunching on the ice-covered grass.

The hum became louder, more distinct as David made progress across the field, his eyes scouring the dark horizon for a clue to its origin. Then he saw it. A large, dull, black thing that just hovered, hovering about two and a half feet above the centre of the field. He had only known it was there when he noticed something was obscuring the starlight.

Moving closer, ever closer, David strained his eyes to take in as much detail as he could. Domed and disc-shaped, he estimated the object was about twenty five feet across and twenty feet high. Antennae or stabilisers poked out from it and there was a drawbridge-like hatchway and windows at the top. He couldn't see any obvious lighting but the object seemed to have a dull, almost muted, fluorescent glow.

Standing there in the cold and darkness, peering at this strange, humming thing floating above the ground and blocking out the starlight, David's attention was caught by a movement off to one side. Switching his gaze, he saw a group of smaller shapes making their way across the field towards him. A group of people, man-like shapes, were making determined progress in his direction. He was overcome by the instinct to flee.

But when he turned to do so he was too late. Another strange humanoid shape was blocking his only escape route. Frozen to the ground, David felt a hand-like grip on his arm and suddenly he was being propelled forwards towards the strange floating object.

'They spoke to me, but not like a person speaking,' recalled David later. 'It was like they were talking to me in my head. They were saying you're all right, you are okay.'

David was transported forwards, his feet not seeming to touch the ground. He is not sure how he entered the object but he found himself in a large bare room where his captors left him alone.

As he waited there, his mind went over the detail he had gathered on his abductors from close range. They were definitely humanoid in shape and were wearing what looked like octagonal helmets which were featureless apart from two dim lights positioned where their eyes should have been.

They wore grey suits with gold-coloured belts and straps that looked similar to braces, black knee boots and gloves.

Watching them as he had approached the craft, David thought they reminded him of something he had seen in the past. Then the similarity struck him. They were like the robots that he had often seen in fifties' Hollywood sci-fi movies. Perhaps it was the way they moved their arms and legs in a rapid, stilted fashion.

David estimates he was kept alone in that bare room for some fifteen minutes. He is convinced that he was under observation by his captors, whether this was assumed on his part, or telepathically communicated to him he is unsure. But throughout his experience he was constantly aware of voices in his head.

For reasons he still can't explain, David was not overcome by fear during his time on the craft, although he would certainly suffer terrors from it later.

After observation, David was led into what he describes as a control room. Three or four TV consoles were visible and a large screen was positioned on a wall. He believes the beings let him know that he was being decontaminated and then prepared for a time change. This information also seemed to be transmitted by some form of telepathy.

David was then aware of the craft taking off. 'But there was no sense of motion at all,' he said. 'I was just sitting there watching this big screen showing planets passing by, Jupiter, Saturn and out to beyond Pluto where the craft docked with a mother ship.'

On board the larger craft David remembers being taken for a medical examination. As he lay on the examination table, positioned in the centre of a room, one of his captors produced a long instrument which was pointed at one end. He believes that instrument was responsible for burn marks which he claims he found on his body the following day.

'It didn't feel like a burn at the time,' David told investigators. 'I didn't realise that is what they were doing until I saw the marks the next day.'

David was confused by one aspect of the medical examination. He explained: 'They checked me all over but they seemed to ponder over my private parts for a while. I don't know whether they were trying to work out whether I was male or female.'

Probes were placed on David's head and chest and around his neck. He remembers his heart rate being increased and then decreased, as if on command from his abductors. He also recalls a bizarre telepathic request. Could they have permission to remove his eyes for further examination? He refused, of course.

A music tape cassette was removed from his pocket by one of the beings and apparently analysed in one of the consoles in the room. David recalls the irony of hearing a very earthy heavy rock anthem pounding out its beat across this most alien of scenes.

He is convinced that in a further telepathic conversation the aliens told him that they came from a planet beyond the constellation of Lyra, that they breathed pure oxygen and disliked the polluted atmosphere of the earth.

They had a temporary base in Greenland and had been forced to destroy a number of bases which had existed on the moon to avoid discovery by probes and visits from earth. They told David that their studies of our planet were conducted on the basis on non interference.

How they reconciled abduction with a policy of non interference was not volunteered.

David told investigators that he was questioned about the USA and NASA and recalls being told that the aliens had captured a Voyager spacecraft for analysis. Their verdict: very primitive.

David is not clear at what point he was taken back to the UFO from the mother ship, but he was aware that he was being taken back home. He suddenly found himself back in that lonely field in North Wales. His last recollection is of the UFO disappearing from view in the night sky.

He vividly recalls experiencing a feeling of dizziness after leaving the alien craft followed by a floating feeling which he assumed could have been caused by breathing a more oxygen-rich atmosphere.

The young man was spotted reeling in the road by a passing police patrol car. The police officer stopped his vehicle and quizzed David, asking him if he'd been drinking or taking drugs. Satisfied that he was not breaking the law, the patrolman took David home where they arrived at 5.30 a.m.

The one hour fifteen minute journey on foot from his friend's home had taken twice as long, even with a lift from the police officer. But he had been with those unearthly visitors for what seemed hours.

As soon as he got home David was gripped by a terror, perhaps a delayed reaction from his traumatic encounter. Although now safe, in the bosom of his family, he was still in a state of shock.

After hearing his account, his mother agreed that they should seek help to try to find out exactly what had happened to him, to help fill in the gaps in his memory.

Two days later they tracked down the phone number of Contact International, the only UFO investigation group they could find.

Yes, Contact were interested in looking at the case, they were told, and would be in touch.

The Thomas family waited just seven days before David's mum, worried by the violent nightmares her son was now suffering, decided to act. At one in the morning on 17th February 1985, she ushered the youngster into the family car for the long journey to the Oxfordshire HQ of Contact.

When they got to their destination they waited in their parked car for dawn to break before seeking out an investigator. David, described as pale, dishevelled and shaking with fear, had to be cajoled by his mother into relating his story. He did so reluctantly, reinforcing his wish for anonymity and refusing point blank to talk to the police or the media.

An ordinary young lad, David was bright and articulate, not prone to flights of fancy, with nothing to gain by fabricating such a story. He had no abiding interest in UFOs and appeared not to have been contaminated by abduction literature.

He seemed stable and in no way an attention seeker, yet he was overcome by fear.

It took investigators several interviews to establish the reason for this terror, which threatened to overshadow this young man's life.

Then during one interview session David confided the one telepathic conversation with his abductors that filled him with dread. They made it plain that they would return to earth again, one day in the future and would seek him out.

'We will see you again,' they told him.

'They have chosen me, they have instructed me and they are coming back for me,' said David, his horror plainly etched on his face.

The investigators pointed out that it was highly unlikely he would have a second encounter and they pointed out the ambiguity of the words used by the beings. Perhaps it was merely a way of saying farewell.

It was impossible to placate the youth whose nightmares continued to plague him. His family were well used to him waking in the night in a cold sweat, his blood-curdling screams rousing the whole household.

David's distress was such that his mother contacted a psychologist who decided that he should undergo hypno-therapy. After a course of such sessions David was able to come to terms with his encounter. He knew he had to pick up the pieces of his life and carry on. He could not live in fear for the rest of his days.

Today David is happily married and has put his abduction experience firmly behind him. So firmly that he refuses to discuss the incident under any circumstances. He also keeps to himself his views on UFOs and abduction phenomena.

But, as he once pointed out when being interviewed by investigators, the experience has changed him.

When they asked him what he had learned from his encounter, the then much younger David said: 'We humans are supposed to be big aren't we? But we're just very small. Insignificant.

'And why do humans want to destroy everything that is good about our world? It makes you think.'

David is now an avid campaigner for Green issues – and he's also developed a talent for song writing and spontaneous poetry.

One of the first poems he penned after his encounter had an intriguing title: 'The Atom'.

Researchers who have investigated the Thomas case over the years unanimously agree that it is a classic. Not just because of the chain of events he reported experiencing, but because of the quality of the witness concerned.

An unemployed teenager a quality witness?

'As a rule of thumb the emotional content of a case is more important than the actual events experienced,' said one investigator who had spent a great many hours interviewing the witness. 'The emotional content of this case was compelling.'

'I have interviewed David twice over the years, once shortly after the event and again some years later. The fear in this young man's face could not be faked.

'When I first went to North Wales to see him I could talk to him about any subject and he would respond quite happily. He was perfectly rational, totally at ease. Then as soon as I raised the subject of his experience he changed dramatically.

'He would fidget, chain smoke, wring his hands. The body language was of a young man in total terror.

'I will never forget the fear in those eyes. You could almost see the beads of sweat break out on his forehead as I coaxed and sometimes bullied him into telling me the details.

'He was also very embarrassed about his new interest in poetry, so much so that he made me swear not to tell his friends about it.'

David's reaction to the subject was just the same when he underwent a further interview some years after his encounter.

'By this time he had undergone hypnotherapy to help him overcome the nightmares and attacks of the terrors.

'He was older, more mature and had made a conscious decision to leave the incident in the past. He really did not want to talk about it. But when I began asking him about details of events his eyes were filled with terror. He changed completely from a relaxed, self-assured young man to a total bag of nerves. David Thompson was not faking.

'I am convinced that he believes the events that he described really did happen to him. Those events terrified him and probably still haunt him today.

'You can't fake the sort of trauma that requires hypnotherapy to treat it.'

THE CHASE

Sightings of strange lights, slices of missing time and vague recollections of alien shapes and scenes? Are these really enough to point to alien abduction? Even when the credibility of the witness is beyond reproach couldn't their reports be explained by some sort of temporary mental condition?

Could the band of pressure felt by Elsie Oakensen around her head be a clue? Was there a physiological explanation for the events she thinks she experienced? Was that pain a symptom of something going on inside her head rather than in outer space?

She herself seems to favour a spiritual explanation.

And Graham Allen's missing time could simply be put down to getting lost during a freak summer downpour. Was the dream of seven years later really that significant? Of course it is possible to pick holes in every story. But an experienced investigator would have asked himself the very same questions that would occur to the cynic. And he would have answered them satisfactorily before going on with the investigation.

No, there was no evidence that Elsie Oakensen's bands of pressure were symptomatic of any illness. And what about the four Women's Institute ladies who sighted a similar object.

No, Graham Allen was quite sure his missing time experience was more than just getting lost. He knew the area too well to have gone astray. And he believes the experience seven years later was significant. Hadn't his wife and children been awoken by the strange humming that night?

With so many question marks cropping up the seasoned investigator of abduction phenomena often asks witnesses to undergo hypnosis. Hypnotic regression has been a favoured tool of Ufologists since the Betty and Barney Hill case in America in the sixties. It had been argued that testimony given under hypnosis could not be faked and that those accounts were a valuable piece of additional evidence.

However in 1977 American Alvin Lawson set up an experiment to test the reliability of hypnosis accounts. First he gathered together a group of people who claimed a genuine UFO abduction experience, had them hypnotically regressed and asked them to give an account of their experience.

At the same time he also gathered a second group of people who were given a basic outline of abduction and then asked to fake an account from their imagination. This second group were then hypnotically regressed and were asked for their account of abduction.

Astonishingly much of the detail given by the imaginary abductees matched the detail of real reports and suggested, at the very least, that those who wish to fake reports under hypnosis had the capacity to do so.

The 'fake' abductees' account were interesting in that they produced a great deal of imaginary information which had not been given by the examiners.

Lawson's experiments were criticised on the basis that in the 1970s in California there would be few people who would not have knowledge of the UFO phenomenon. While this is true, these days many who claim the genuine abduction experience will have some knowledge, inevitably, of UFOs.

There is one major difference, however, between the recall of the genuine abductee and those who imagine abduction: emotional response. The genuine abductees display considerable emotion during recall, while the imaginary abductees relate their account as if describing a TV programme they have seen.

However, said researchers, this merely indicates that those who claim genuine experience also genuinely believe it to have happened and are therefore potentially frightened of it, whereas those who do not claim the experience have nothing to fear. But, they say, the belief of an individual does not necessarily reflect the reality of the experience.

Other studies have also cast considerable doubt on the reliability of accounts given by subjects while in hypnotic trance.

Hypnosis can be a dangerous tool in the wrong hands and if used on the wrong subject can cause problems. For that reason, and because of the doubts about the validity of the testimony gathered under this procedure, BUFORA imposed a moratorium on hypnotic regression several years ago, and that ban remains today.

Experience had shown that it was not always easy to persuade witnesses or potential abductees to go through with what some can find a harrowing ordeal, and when they do the results can be disappointing.

But in the case of Christine Smith the results were astounding.

Christine Smith (pseudonym),
4 March 1982,
Skipton,
North Yorkshire.

It was about 10.15 p.m. on the night of Thursday 4th March 1982 when the logical, rational workaday world of Christine Smith fell apart.

The thirty-six year old mother of two and businesswoman had spent a pleasant day with her mum in Morecambe and was driving home to Skipton, North Yorkshire unaware that the events that were about to follow would force her to reappraise her view of life and her understanding of the universe.

Alone in her car apart from the family sheep dog which slept on the floor on the front passenger side, Christine bowled along the quiet country roads at a steady 50 miles per hour.

She hardly noticed the rugged moorland terrain that stretched for miles around her as she motored through the Lancashire and Yorkshire borderlands on what was a cold clear night.

The moon shone brightly in a sky full of stars as her car coasted along the A65 to complete the final leg of the 50 mile journey she had undertaken many times before.

Her mind was full of the household chores that needed attending to before she could get to bed and rest in preparation for the next day's work in the family business.

As she approached lonely Coniston Cutting, not far from Skipton, where the road slices through a large hill creating steep banks on either side of the carriageway, she was passed by a single car coming from the opposite direction. She watched through her rear view mirror as its lights slowly disappeared into the distance.

Drivers through this vast expanse of moorland know that from Coniston Cutting one can see vehicle headlights for a considerable distance in both directions. And that night, at that moment, Christine felt as if her car was the only one in existence as it purred on through the night.

Suddenly, from the corner of her eye, she was aware of a light coming from one side of her car. She turned and saw that the whole of the offside of her vehicle seemed illuminated with a soft bluish light.

It was then that she glanced in her offside wing mirror and saw the two lights; two strange lights positioned behind and just above the height of her car.

About the same size as car head lamps, one was royal blue and the other a vivid red. They seemed to be tailing her car, lights side by side with the red light on the outside. Noticing they were bright, yet somehow soft, Christine at times thought she could see a number of smaller lights behind them. She peered through her rear view mirror and all was blackness. Then she glanced again in the wing mirror and there they were.

She discarded the idea that they were odd headlights from a large lorry which had somehow caught up with her. They were too high, the wrong colour . . .

Whatever they were they didn't seem to bother the dog who slept on unaware of his mistress's growing sense of unease.

'Pull yourself together girl,' she told herself determined to concentrate on her driving. She only had a handful of miles to cover.

As her car emerged from the cutting, Christine's sense of relief was replaced by sheer terror. A beam of pure white light shot down from somewhere above and illuminated the road at the nearside of her vehicle.

A circle of light, more than fifteen feet in diameter, first fell onto the fields, then moved onto the road. Suddenly the car was encircled by this girdle of bright energy.

'I suddenly felt very cold,' she said later. 'I knew *that* in itself was strange because the car heater was on.'

She also experienced the eerie silence that is often reported by close encounter witnesses. It was an unnatural absence of sound, except for the engine noise. This seemed to be revving far louder than it should have been.

Christine was determined to press on and drew on all her resources to keep driving, keep concentrating despite knowing that the lights were still behind her.

For what seemed like eternity she kept at bay what she described as the urge to slam on the brakes, scream and bury her head in her hands. Yet later she realised the beam can only have paced her car for a distance of half a mile at the most.

It was the sudden appearance of the headlights from an approaching large lorry in the distance that jerked her back to something more like reality. At the exact second that the heavy vehicle's head lamps appeared on the horizon the beam flicked out and her red and blue pursuers vanished.

Still gripped by a terror that they would return Christine summoned up what strength she had left to complete the journey. The fear began to subside as her vehicle passed the familiar buildings and landmarks on the outskirts of Skipton that told her that home, and safety, were not far away.

As she parked up outside her home she was filled with a huge sense of relief, yet she felt mentally and physically drained from her ordeal. That feeling of complete exhaustion would stay with her for a further week, an indication of the traumatic effect her journey had on her.

Christine's husband Gerry shared a feeling of relief as he let his wife in. He had been worried for her safety. It was now after 11 p.m . . . .one hour and thirty five minutes after Christine had left her mother's home.

The journey which normally took an hour, had not been hampered by traffic and after seeing the disturbed state she was in he was anxious to hear her story.

Gerry had no problem accepting Christine's account. This well-spoken, intelligent businesswoman had been visibly shaken by her experience; she was not a UFO freak and had never been prone to concocting fantastic stories.

Alarmingly, the following day Christine found she had a rash on her back and chest, unusual for her, but it cleared up in a couple of days.

As word of the encounter spread among friends of the couple one mentioned it to a colleague associated with UFO research. He immediately contacted Christine who agreed to relate her account on condition it was not publicised and that her identity be kept confidential.

Once this was agreed Christine went through the detailed telling and re-telling of the experience as the investigator noted every single detail. Christine's version of events never wavered.

As time went on the Ufologist was convinced that he had an abductee. The lights, the malfunctioning of the car and the missing time pointed to a Close Encounter of the Fourth Kind.

Hypnotism was the obvious next step and the investigator was delighted when Christine agreed. But he had no idea how delighted he would be with the results of a series of hypnosis sessions which began on 4 May 1982.

Immediately after being put into a trance new material began to emerge. Christine's account of events under hypnosis not only underlined the accuracy of her conscious recollections but brought to light aspects that she had either forgotten or buried away in her mind as inexplicable.

Hypnosis also enabled her to 'remember' what can only be described as an apparent conversation with an alien being.

The hypnotherapist first put Christine into a deep trance and invited her to allow her mind to go back to that fateful night. For all intents and purposes Christine was back in the driver's seat of her car. She described in detail the appearance of lights . . . and some new and interesting detail.

 H: Can your hear anything?
 C: A soft buzzing.
 H: How do you feel?
 C: Very cold all over.
 H: How are you feeling.
 C: I feel so very tired. I want to go to sleep.
 (Her head lolls over to one side as if asleep.)
 H: How do you feel?
 C: I can feel something soft and fluffy on my ankles and feet
 H: Does it hurt?
 C: No, it feels quite nice really. There's a tingling feeling
  going up my legs towards my knees.

When the hypnotist asked her if she was still in the car, Christine replied that she didn't know. She was unsure where she was, unaware of whether she was sitting or lying. But she could hear what sounded like heavy breathing and felt some sort of a veil before her eyes.

H: Could it be a blindfold?

C: It could be there is a bright light coming through the veil. It is going round and round.

At this point Christine begins to gyrate her body from the waist upwards as if keeping time with a rotating light.

H: Can you still feel the strange fluffy thing on your legs?

C: Yes. It appears to be holding my legs down. I still feel very cold except for my legs. They are warm.

Christine didn't respond to a series of further questions then suddenly put her arms out in front of her, bent at the elbow.

H: What are you doing

C: I can't move them. Something is holding them. I can feel something touching my body ... I can hear buzzing all around me.

The first session of hypnosis ended there. It was decided to give Christine a break to prepare her for the next session which took place on 20 May 1982.

Again she was taken back to the point where she spotted the lights and again new information was unearthed.

Under hypnosis she recalled feeling something being placed in the small of her back while she was still in the car. 'Take it away, it hurts,' she cried without identifying who she was speaking to.

Suddenly the 'rotating lights' were back. Putting her hands over her head she called: 'My cheeks are hot, my hands are hot. Whatever it is, it's above the car ...'

Christine's mood changed suddenly. She began humming, then laughing. Her hands had begun tingling, she said, laughing out loud.

C: It's a funny, funny feeling creeping over me.'

H: Can you feel anything in the small of your back?

C: No, not at the moment, I did have before. I've told them to take it away.

H: Told who?
C: Don't know.

At this point Christine complained of a strange feeling in her head, a feeling of pressure. 'It's a square there,' she said, indicating a spot between her eyes.

A band of pressure around her head followed and now, after further questions about the lights and the beam, Christine says her arms 'feel funny'. With her hands out in front of her she makes as if feeling for something.

H: What can you see?.
C: I don't know, it's very dark.'

She reveals feeling as if she is lying down, she feels something warm nearby.

C: They're wanting information.
H: What kind of information?
They can have all they want.
(Christine bursts into loud laughter.)
C: They think that's funny.
H: So they have a sense of humour then?
C: Oh yes. They don't trust us . . .

At this point the investigator asks some pointed questions.

Investigator: Where are they from?
C: Distant galaxy.
I: Where do they live?
C: Zircon, something like that.
I: Will they show themselves?
C: They say they want to be like a friend . . . .
I: Are you important to them?
C: Yes, yes, yes. Oh yes.
I: Because you are a woman?
C: It helps.
I: Why?
C: We can communicate better.

Christine describes how the 'aliens' have many ways of

communication, how they are so advanced, how they protect us. 'They're just guardians, they're good' she said.

> I: How long have they been coming here?
> C: Centuries.
> I: Are they our Gods?
> C: We call them such.
> I: We do?
> C: Since time immemorial, we call them many names.
> I: What names?
> C: Zeus, it's the first name, Akaber.

Christine then told how the 'Guardians', for want of a better name, had been visiting earth to offer help. She said they told her that they could give assistance through 'special powers'.

> I: Who are they accountable to?
> C: A force greater than them.
> I: God?
> C: We call him that.

During the rest of this four hour session under hypnosis Christine spoke of good and evil forces at work about the future of earth and some vague threat to the planet. Exhausted she was brought out of her trance state and immediately agreed to a further session.

The third and final session began as the previous ones, taking Christine back to her night on the road. Suddenly she sat up with her head held high. Confused the investigator asked:

> Are we talking to Christine?
> C: I am Christine, you are talking to Zeus
> I: Ask him how he travels from his distant galaxy?
> C: By beam of light.
> I: Does he travel by machine?
> C: Over long distances.
> I: How fast does his machine go?
> C: As fast as he requires . . . the pressure is pushing down.
> I: Is it painful?
> C: No, it's very heavy.

I: Are you experiencing fear?
C: No
I: Is Zircon the name of their planet?
C: They say we do not know it.
I: Ask them if life ends at death.
C: No.
I: If Zeus is a God should we worship him?
C: No.
I: Can you name other Gods?
C: There are many Gods, they are an all-involved power.
I: If Zeus has a name the other Gods must have names?
C: Narcias is the name coming to me.

The investigator got a shock when he asked about reports of visitors to witnesses at other UFO incidents. Christine's response was almost vehement.

I: They are not of this world. They are evil, evil, evil.

Asked for a demonstration of proof Christine replied: 'In our own time.'

I: Are we speaking to one entity or more?
C: You are speaking to Zeus

A reliable, credible witness, a bizarre series of events and an intriguing series of hypnosis sessions.

The events on that lonely night-time drive, the strange lights and the chase were odd enough in themselves. Combined with the missing time this case certainly had the ingredients of an abduction.

Then the hypnotic regression leads on to a bizarre question and answer session with an alien called Zeus.

Another classic in Abduction Phenomena? A rare insight into the unknown? Or is it another case of gobbledygook with about as much basis in fact as ghouls and goblins.

Despite the reservations about hypnosis, serious researchers say there are some interesting details in this case. Again the quality of the witness, or abductee, means it is worthy of serious consideration.

It was tempting to suspect contamination in view of Christine's references to Gods and indeed Zeus. Had she read Erich von Daniken's Chariots of the Gods? If she had couldn't seeds of information about that theory have remained buried in her brain, lying dormant until being awakened by hypnosis.

Not according to Christine and her husband. She hadn't read von Daniken and his theories were completely unknown to her.

But the theory that advanced alien visitations could have explained the miracle-making Gods of ancient history has been put forward by a number of people in books, films and TV shows that Christine may have glimpsed over the years.

So if Christine's case was not manna from Heaven it must surely be food for thought.

OFFICIAL RECOGNITION

What on earth is going on out there? Even focusing on the alleged alien abduction material from the UK alone, it is clear that something very strange is happening.

When you consider the many thousands of cases from around the world it seems incredible that there has been no concerted, authoritative, global scientific investigation into this phenomenon.

Ignore the millions of alleged UFO sightings and close encounters, what we are dealing with here are alleged abductions of human beings. People are reporting being carried off for examination and tested by beings who seem able to flout the law at will.

Even if you ignore the reports from Third World countries or far flung places where alleged alien abduction is regarded as having little consequence when a society is struggling to feed itself, there are enough cases in America and Europe to justify a real scientific examination.

But even in America, where UFO organisations have influential names and money behind them, they have been unable to get their Government to launch a proper investigation.

Early in spring 1994 British cynics showed their true colours when they noisily debunked a European Community suggestion to set up a UFO research programme . With that level of cynicism, a research programme into abduction phenomenon is obviously a non starter.

Yet abductions, if true, are far more serious than lights in the sky. Many of those people are damaged psychologically if not physically. And it remains to be seen whether the reasons behind these events are sinister or otherwise

So why are our abductees not taken seriously? We have demonstrated in the few cases that we have looked at so far, that the witnesses are credible. They have nothing to gain and much to lose by exposing themselves to ridicule. However, the circumstantial evidence is just not compelling enough for it to warrant a serious investigation.

Perhaps the major reason for the general reluctance to recognise abduction phenomenon is that in all the material available in a great many recorded cases world-wide, one vital ingredient is missing: the stamp of authority.

Find a case with a credible witness, where an alleged alien visitation leaves some form of mark on the environment, where there is some physical evidence of an attempt at abduction and with some supporting involvement by the authorities, such as the police, then you might make some people sit up and take notice, or so the theory goes.

It is not always so, as Robert Taylor discovered.

Robert Taylor,
9 November 1979,
Livingston,
Scotland.

Foreman forester Robert Taylor was sixty one when he almost became the victim of a Close Encounter of the Fourth Kind. Only a combination of his Scottish stubbornness and good luck meant he could claim to be *the one that got away.*

So credible a witness was he and so graphic his description of events that the police and other authorities launched a full investigation. Although the case did not go down in the annals of police history as 'assault with a deadly UFO', the official investigation provided a catalogue of evidence from a number of truly independent observers – the boys in blue.

In fact fifteen years on Robert has become such a local legend that a memorial has been erected on the site of his encounter with a UFO . . . .the only such official commemoration in existence connected to a flying saucer landing.

Robert needs no help in recalling that winter's morning in 1979.

To the married father of five grown-up children it was just another working day with the Forestry Department of the Livingston New Town Development Corporation in Scotland.

He had just enjoyed his usual breakfast break at the house he shared with his wife Mary at Deans, just outside Livingston, and climbed into his pick-up truck for the short drive to inspect some forest plantations at Dechmont Wood near the M8 motorway which links Glasgow to Edinburgh.

A punctual man, Robert left his home shortly after 10 a.m. and headed off, knowing that he would have to make the last leg of his journey on foot as the rough forest track was impassable to vehicles.

At 10.15 a.m. he left the truck parked by the side of the road and, accompanied by his dog, set off through the rough woodland vegetation on the half mile trek that would take him to his destination.

Robert had worked on the land all his life and had been with the Livingston Forestry Department for the last sixteen years, so there was not much he did not know about this patch of bonny Scotland for which he was responsible.

But as he rounded a bend in the rough forest track, Robert was totally unprepared for what would confront him in the clearing ahead.

A thirty feet high dome-shaped object, grey in colour, lay before him. Dominating the clearing, the strange mass, silent yet ominous, caused him to stop in his tracks.

Mesmerised, Robert noted how its surface seemed to become translucent and then changed back to a dull grey, the same colour and apparent texture as emery paper, he thought. For some reason he found himself wondering whether this bizarre machine, if machine it was, was trying to camouflage itself.

What he later described as a 'flange' girdled the strange structure, and antenna-like protrusions with, what could have been rotors on top, jutted out from the flange at regular intervals.

Transfixed to the ground at the end of the thirty yard wide clearing Robert's eyes scoured the surface of the massive object trying to make some sense of it. He noted several round porthole-type apertures in the top section of the dome.

It was while he was absorbed by the portholes, the 'sea mines' appeared. That was how Robert described the two objects which suddenly came at him, apparently from thin air.

Spherical and with six or more legs or spikes protruding from them, they rapidly rolled towards him. Measuring about a yard in diameter, and of the same colour and texture as the larger object, the sea mines made a sucking or popping sound as each spike or leg touched the ground.

Within seconds they had stationed themselves at either side of the now stunned forestry worker, each having a spike or leg attached to the material of his trousers.

Immediately, Robert could feel himself being pulled forward, the spheres tugging him by his trousers, urging him in the direction of the large object.

He could see the material of his trousers, just below the pockets, straining under the powerful pull of the spikes or the legs. Robert stubbornly resisted them. He wasn't going to run away but he would certainly try to stand his ground against this invader.

The spheres steadily increased their pull to such an extent that at one stage Robert could feel his wellington boots dragging on the ground as he fought to keep his distance from the gloomy grey object.

A foul acrid smell that he had noticed as soon as the spheres approached now seemed to fill his nostrils. The intensity of the appalling stench increased as he struggled with his would be captors. Invisible choking fumes overwhelmed him as he summoned all his strength to resist the incessant pull of the spheres.

A strange pressure built up under his chin and he recalls a burning sensation in the same place.

Struggling for breath and exhausted from his battle with 'sea mines', Robert lost consciousness and fell forward into the damp grass.

'The next thing I hear a whooshing sound and my dog is racing around me barking loudly,' remembers Robert. 'But I'm not sure if that was before I lost consciousness or after I came round.

'When I did come round there was nothing there. The object had gone. I felt extremely weak and was unsteady on my feet. I dragged myself up and half crawled, half staggered to my vehicle.'

On reaching his pick-up truck Robert automatically went to his two-way radio to report the incident to HQ. But as soon as they responded he found he could not utter a word. He could not speak.

But losing his voice was the least of his worries. After climbing, with some effort, into the driver's seat of his truck, Robert struggled to co-ordinate his hand and leg movements to enable him to drive.

After several attempts he managed to start the vehicle and steer it along the forest track for a few yards before it went veering into a muddy quagmire. Dazed and confused, Robert made his way home on foot. Gradually his strength, and his voice returned.

Mary, his wife, saw her husband walking up the road

towards his home through the kitchen window. She noticed his face was dirty and his clothes dishevelled.

Rushing out to meet him she cried: 'What's happened? Have you had an accident?'

'No, I've been attacked,' he replied.

'By men?'

'No, a spaceship thing.'

'There's no such thing . . . I'll phone the doctor.'

Robert stopped his wife calling the GP and asked her to run him a bath. He wanted to get rid of the awful smell that he believed clung to him and his clothes.

Mary could not smell a thing but she did notice his jersey was dirty. And his trousers were torn on either side near to the pockets as well as being grubby at the front. He had obviously fallen.

Mary could see her husband was unwell. He was very pale. He seemed drained and exhausted and complained of grazes on his left leg and under his chin.

While he was in the bath, Mary telephoned her husband's boss, Malcolm Drummond, the forestry manager. When he arrived at the house Robert told his story, describing the domed object as like a large spinning top, accompanied by two smaller objects.

Mr Drummond listened without interruption. He knew old Robert was a man of few words, not one for exaggeration. If this is what he said had happened then he was prepared to believe him.

Mr Drummond said he was going to look at the site for himself and left. When he returned he brought back Robert's truck and said that despite a cursory look around the location, he had nothing to report. Robert insisted on returning to Dechmont Wood with his boss to see if the object had left any marks on the ground. There must be some sign of it having been there.

Indeed marks there were, and they were enough to convince Robert that he had not imagined his experience. Track-like marks and holes, three inches deep and at a slight angle into the ground. They suggested a heavy object had been sitting there. Mr Drummond had to agree they were strange. The police were immediately called in to investigate.

In his report on the incident PC William Douglas of Lothian and Borders Police at Livingston described the marks in detail:

> The central marks were similar to that of a caterpillar tractor and were uniform in size. They indicated that an object of several tons had stood there but there was nothing to show that it had been driven or towed away.
>
> I made a wide sweep of the area checking for fresh marks which might suggest a mobile crane but I found nothing.
>
> The central marks were surrounded by holes approximately 3.5 inches in diameter and the same in depth. Each hole had a toe which cut under the sod, in some cases by as much as four inches. There appeared to be no rational explanation for these marks.

PC Douglas's search for signs of a mobile crane implied that he thought the object, whatever it was, must have been lifted from the spot. An object, weighing several tons, according to his estimation, would certainly have left further marks when it moved off.

The official report by the Livingston Criminal Investigation Department concluded:

> Despite extensive inquiries made, no information has been gained which could indicate what, in fact, made the marks on the ground at the location. Mr Taylor is a respected member of the community and is described as a conscientious and trustworthy person, not likely to invent a story.

The police investigation included a report from the Forensic Science Laboratory, where Robert's clothing had undergone testing. Nothing of significance was found. But the report confirmed that the tears in the hip area of the trousers he had been wearing, and in a corresponding area on the Long John underpants favoured by Robert, were 'consistent with the material having been pulled up while the trousers were being worn'.

The report from Robert's GP, Dr Gordon Adams, was equally inconclusive. He found no signs of a head injury or concussion. He had seen him earlier in the year when it was suspected that headaches he was suffering could be a return of the meningitis he had some fourteen years previously. However hospital tests ruled this out.

The flurry of press reports of Robert's experience were mostly the tongue-in-cheek *Forestry Worker Meets Alien* type; the media is at least always consistent in handling such stories.

Another observer at the scene at the time explained away the incident as an encounter with ball lightning. But Robert is hardly likely to have mistaken this natural phenomenon for the object he described in such detail and it certainly cannot account for the very physical effects of his encounter.

But the British UFO Research Association's own files throw up some interesting sightings from the same area and at about the same time as Robert's meeting with his 'spinning top thing'.

The evening before, Peter Caldwell, a thirty five year old clerk at a factory at nearby Uphall, saw a dull, white, round object travelling from west to east across the sky. Behind it was a large red patch 'as if the air was on fire'.

That same evening postman James Forsyth saw two white lights pass in the sky above him. First they approached each other, then passed, then approached and passed yet again as James walked his dog through a park in the Craigmillar area of Edinburgh.

At 9.30 a.m., possibly on the same day as Robert's encounter, an Edinburgh woman reported a bright light in the sky travelling west, towards Livingston. She described it as dull, white grey in colour with 'neither wings nor tail'.

Mrs Barbara Gerrard of Leslie in Fife, saw three orange/pink lights in the sky on the afternoon of 9th November, and at 10 a.m. on the same day thirty five year Violet Connor of nearby Bathgate saw a bright light in the sky to the west, over Armadale, which is just across the M8 from Livingston.

Robert Taylor's encounter baffled the Development Corporation of Livingston, the police, the medics, his wife and most of all himself. It still sparks fierce debate among Ufologists.

Were the occupants of the UFO trying to abduct Robert? He believes they were and fought back. Is he sure it was a UFO?

Robert is convinced and neither the police nor the other authorities have been able to come up with an alternative explanation. And as far as other witnesses are concerned, couldn't at least one of those people making sighting reports to BUFORA over that period have seen the same object that Robert encountered?

Happily Robert, now in his seventies and still pleased to recount his event, has not faced the sneering ridicule that many witnesses have experienced. In fact he has achieved something of celebrity status in his local community. So much so that local councillors voted to erect a *cairn* or monument to the Close Encounter at Livingston.

Erected in May 1992 the commemorative plaque and *cairn* were the result of a collaboration between the Livingston Development Corporation and the Scottish UFO research group Strange Phenomena Investigations.

THE AVELEY CASE

The vast majority of Abduction Phenomena reports come from individuals who have experienced strange events without witnesses. But couples and even groups of people have had Close Encounters of the Fourth Kind.

The advantage of the multiple witness experience from the point of view of the investigator is obvious. He has the images seen and mentally recorded by two or more pairs of eyes to rely upon instead of one. He will interview all witnesses separately so that later he can examine the accounts to see if and where they differ.

Images and perceptions will differ to some extent with every individual but multiple witness case accounts will have a large area of common ground.

When two or more people claim to have been abducted, the investigator also has two or more points of reference for considering the authenticity of their report.

However good the lone witness, the critic can always argue that without any physical evidence his account is, by its very nature, subjective.

How do we know that the witness did not undergo some temporary mental impairment in the form of hallucinations? How do we know that he didn't just concoct the story for the fun of it? He could have made up the tale for a bet, or even for an alibi.

The truth is single abduction reports are, for the most part, subjective. We cannot know with absolute certainty that the truth is being told.

Multiple abduction reports, on the other hand, are another matter. Of course two or more people can also concoct an abduction story for the same reasons as above, but it is more likely that their deceptions will be discovered, with two separate accounts of events to check and cross check.

Because more than one person is involved the accounts should become more objective, and, unless we blame mass hallucination, more believable.

Most of these multiple alleged abduction reports come, as always, from the USA and the rest of the world.

But here in Britain we have one of the most well-researched of such case histories. It is known as the Aveley Case.

The alleged abductees in this case were a family of five; John and Sue Day and their three young children.

Their experience still baffles the experts nearly two decades later.

The Day Family,
27 October 1974,
Aveley,
Essex.

A quick glance around the car to make sure everyone was safely in was enough to tell John Day they were ready to go. He switched on the ignition of his Vauxhall Victor estate and began to pull away. His wife Sue leaned out of the front passenger window to say her goodbyes to her parents and sister.

John had been anxious to get on the move. It was still only 9.50 pm and the BBC 2 play he wanted to watch wouldn't start for another half an hour. If the traffic wasn't too bad they would manage the trip home to Aveley in twenty minutes giving them just enough time to get the kids to bed and put on the kettle before settling down in front of the television.

'Hush,' cooed Sue as she leaned awkwardly around to tend to the two youngsters who had already fallen asleep on the back seat of the car. Karen, eleven, and seven year old Stuart had been exhausted by their day at the home of Sue's mum and dad at Harold Hill.

They had made the trip to welcome home Sue's sister Anne who had just returned from a week's trip to Belgium. But she was four hours late and John was cursing his bad luck in the way that only Cockneys can.

At least he would still have the chance to see the play, he told Sue as he leaned forward to switch on the car radio. It was a local station chat show.

John was aware of ten year old Kevin standing behind him as he steered his car along the familiar route through Hornchurch.

'Not much traffic about, is there luv?' he said glancing over at his wife.

She didn't answer, content to enjoy the beautiful clear night. It was mild and dry. A lovely night for a drive.

About a mile from Hornchurch and heading south as they made their way along the section of the road which has terraced houses on one side and fields bordered with tall edges on the other, Kevin asked: 'What's that light?'

Following Kevin's outstretched arm John and Sue spotted it immediately. Just above the terraced houses on their left. It was an oval shape, a bluish iridescent light, like a big star. But it appeared to be no more than fifty yards away.

'Look, it's moving,' said Kevin.

'Yeah, and it keeps stopping and starting,' said his dad.

Sue asked her husband if he thought it could be a helicopter light, but he pointed out that they would have been able to hear the engine, and anyway it wouldn't move like that.

Seconds later the light was obscured by a small wood which the car was passing. When it came into view again it was still travelling in the same direction and at the same speed.

Suddenly the object changed course and approached the road they were travelling along. It picked up speed and zipped across them at a steep angle.

John pushed down on the brake, slowed the car and pressed his head close to the windscreen to try to get a better view of the strange object, but this time it was obscured by some high bushes.

The road then took them into a dip and after a bend to the right became Aveley Road. Pressing on for another mile or so they passed a gravel pit and several bungalows before approaching another curve. John checked his speed, thirty mph, no need to change down before negotiating the bend.

Suddenly he was gripped by a sense of panic. Something was terribly wrong. Sue looked across at her husband, fear in her eyes. The engine had stopped. No, it was just silent. They were still moving, the radio was playing normally, but they couldn't hear the sound of the engine.

As the car came out of the bend it plunged into a bank of fog or thick mist, although John remembers it seemed more like gas. Dense and green, the eerie fog bank was about eight or nine feet high, completely enveloping the car.

The swirling vapour seemed to start from a line of thick bushes that bordered the road on the left and swept down to the ground on the right in what looked like a perfect curve.

Suddenly the car radio began crackling loudly and when John spotted smoke drifting up out of the apparatus he quickly leaned over and wrenched out a bunch of wires from the back of the set.

At that moment every light in the vehicle blinked out and the car began to jerk violently as the strange green mist curled around them, fingers of fog apparently exploring every square inch of the bodywork for some means of entry.

Windows tightly closed, John continued to drive, at least he kept his foot on the accelerator and gripped the steering wheel, watched by Sue and with little Kevin gripping his dad's shoulders for reassurance. Thankfully Karen and Stuart slept on peacefully through the unfolding drama

Oddly, John and Sue recall no sense of motion during those frightening seconds. However they do remember the car becoming much colder, as if the mist was drawing out every bit of heat from the vehicle.

Despite the fog it seemed light although hazy. Both later remarked on the total silence and experiencing a curious tingling sensation.

With a jolt, as if racing over a hump-back bridge the car was now most definitely on the move. And the mist was gone.

In fact, John estimated they emerged from the mist exactly half a mile along the road from the point they entered it.

John felt as if he was alone in the car until the vehicle had covered maybe another half mile or so when Sue sat up and asked: 'Is everybody here?'

The cold had gone, the car was functioning normally, the interior lights were switched on, but the radio wires were still disconnected, hanging down from behind the dash board.

Nervous and frightened, they spoke quietly about the mist until they reached their home.

While Sue put the children to bed – Stuart and Karen had remained asleep throughout – John busied himself with re-wiring the car radio and then checked if the lights still worked.

Sue joined him, with a puzzled look on her face. She said, 'John, what time do you think it is?'

'About 10.20?'

'No. It's one in the morning.'

Sue had phoned the speaking clock to check the time.

Three hours were missing from their lives and they hadn't a clue how.

John and Sue felt extremely tired the following day, so John decided not to go into work. Exhaustion apart, they seemed to suffer no ill effects.

Some weeks later, however, in the run up to Christmas, John suffered a nervous breakdown. There was no apparent reason, no problems at home, no difficulty at work.

Aged thirty two, John was forced to give up his carpentry job and remained out of work until September the following year when he began a new career, caring for the mentally handicapped.

He and Sue had not forgotton that night of 27 October 1974, but they hadn't approached any organisations for help in investigating the incident because they weren't aware of any such organisations – and anyway they had enough on their plates with John's sudden illness.

Both, however, could not help but notice how their lives had changed since that night. John was more self-confident; he was now apt to writing spur of the moment poems and yearned to begin a new career teaching arts and crafts.

Sue too enjoyed more self-confidence and enrolled at college for further education.

Kevin, the only one of the three children to remain awake during the entire journey, also underwent a remarkable change. From being pronounced backward at reading by his school, he suddenly improved to a level ahead of his years.

In the weeks and months following their encounter the whole family turned vegetarian, John gave up smoking and they all took a fervent interest in Green issues.

Nearly three years after the incident John saw an article about UFOs in his local paper. He decided to contact the local research group to tell them of the strange object he, Sue and Kevin had seen that night.

Investigator Andy Collins came onto the scene in August 1977 and put the whole family through the process of recalling every scrap of information about that night.

Although John and Sue managed to piece together a fairly detailed run down of events during their journey, Andy wanted some clues to the missing three hours.

After quizzing them on dreams and flash-backs they had both experienced Andy was convinced that there was a minefield of information buried in their heads. He asked them to consider hypnosis.

John and Sue were totally unaware that hypnosis could be used to delve for information. And John was so keen to get to the bottom of his experience that he immediately agreed to co-operate.

Sue did not feel ready for such an ordeal and all agreed that Kevin was too young for hypnosis.

Hypnotherapist Leonard Wilder agreed to conduct the hypnotic regression sessions although he had little knowledge of abduction phenomena at that time.

Andy was impatient for the therapy to go ahead. He had a feeling he was on the verge of tapping a wealth of abduction data from the Days. The interview sessions had prompted both John and Sue to volunteer snatches of information they had gleaned in their flash-backs, information they had previously 'forgotten'.

In the first of three hypnosis sessions, Dr Wilder confirmed that John was a good subject. The mass of information from all three bouts of regression combined with the data from other detailed interviews enabled Andy to piece together a remarkable account of events inside the green gas . . . .

A white pillar of light cut through the greenness. John gauged it was just six feet ahead of his car. The weird fog completely engulfed the vehicle yet there was no mistaking it. That strange pillar of light, about four feet in diameter, was definitely moving towards them. The pillar seemed to 'latch on' to the vehicle. Then a feeling of rising, of ascent, as if something were pulling the vehicle upwards.

John blacked out at that point but Sue recalls her head being thrown back and being conscious of Kevin, who had been standing at the rear, falling backwards onto the seat.

Now John was standing on a balcony with a railing in front of him. He was looking down on a large blue car which was apparently on a lower level. Inside he could see a man and a women with her head back, both were unconscious. In the rear there were more bodies, but they were indistinct.

Despite a strong impression that he was looking down at himself and his own family he rationalised that he couldn't be. His car was white, a white Vauxhall Victor.

As he watched, a ramp or a panel began to close in front of the car and he realised then that Sue and Kevin were standing beside him. Behind him was a tall person, an entity, standing perhaps six feet eight inches or so.

To his right, John could see an airshaft, by which, he was certain, he had ascended to that level. It consisted of a cylindrical luminosity between the ground and the balcony. Down on the ground he saw the luminosity end at a hexagonal base.

John and the tall entity moved together towards a blank wall. Suddenly John experienced an ascending motion. A hole appeared in the wall and John walked through into a room containing a table with lights above. The tall being touched him on his shoulder and he was in blackness.

Sue, too, recalled being led away from the balcony towards a blank wall which similarly opened up to reveal an entrance to a room. Two small beings were waiting for her. A tall entity then approached and took hold of Kevin.

Angry that he seemed to want to separate a mother and her son, Sue tightened her hold on the youngster's shoulders. Silently the entity drew the boy towards him, then the child was guided wordlessly into another room.

John regained consciousness to find himself lying on an examination table. He felt as if he were being scanned by a bar which passed over his body. He could feel a tingling sensation and a strange warmth in the area covered by the device.

Five figures stood around the table, three tall entities to the right and two 'ugly looking beings' about four feet in height and wearing white gowns to the left.

He watched as one of the shorter beings, whom he dubbed 'examiners', ran a pen-like object, eight inches long, over his skin. Although it never actually touched his body, it emitted a light and caused a warm, tingling sensation in those parts of the body over which it was held.

John scrutinised the examiner holding the pen-like object. The white gown he wore fell loosely to the ground, the long loose sleeves were drawn in at the cuffs. The being had no neck and appeared to be slightly hunched.

Bushy brown fur, or hair, covered its head and hands; its eyes were large and slanting, triangular in shape. A light-brown nose or beak, a slit for a mouth and pointed ears which swept back completed the picture.

Large talons or nails protruded from the four digits on each of its two very large hands. Thickly set, the being walked awkwardly and occasionally made guttural sounds.

The examiners appeared almost reverential to the tall beings who towered a clear two and a half feet above them. They wore one piece seamless suits of a lurex type material.

The material formed a balaclava shape over the heads of the beings. Their faces, being very different from the 'examiners', comprised two large eyes of a cream colour with pink irises. The absence of a visible nose or mouth suggested they were wearing masks.

John could clearly see their hands of three digits covered by a very pale, almost translucent skin.

Unable to move during the examination, when he felt they had completed their tests John asked if he could get up.

'Sit there for a while.'

As he sat up and swung his legs over the side of the table John realised the reply had not been spoken. Some form of telepathy was involved because he seemed to get a mental impression of what they wanted to say.

From his new vantage point, John had a better view of the room he was in. It was about twenty feet long by twelve feet wide. Vaguely oval in shape, there were no corners or seams. It was like sitting in a bubble. Apart from the table on which he was sitting and the two lights above, the room was bare.

John found himself dressed in a one-piece garment similar to those worn by the tall entities.

Now feeling bolder he began to ask questions.

'What do you do when you're outside the ship?'

'We use a visor,' came the reply. John saw one of the three entities holding out a hemispherical object with two head bands attached. It reminded him of a welder's visor.

The tallest of the beings, the one who seemed to be doing

the communicating, said:' We find this unfortunate (the visor) because we see through your eyes for most purposes.

'There are occasions when we cannot find suitable eyes so we use the visor to change your light to match our optic nerves.'

Encouraged by the response to his first question, John tried a second. 'Why are there no colours on your craft?'

'For you there are not but for us there is colour,' came the reply. 'Because of the structure of our optic unit, the light we receive is interpreted differently. The conditions here are controlled in our favour and that is why you see what you see.'

John then requested a tour of the craft. To his surprise a tall being immediately came forward to lead him to a wall where a hole appeared. Seven feet high and three feet across, the aperture closed as soon as John and the three tall entities passed through. They were in a connecting tunnel which led them to a room similar in size to the examination chamber. It contained couches and a single table upon which were some boxes. John felt this was used for leisure purposes.

Out into the tunnel again and on to the next room went John and the three tall entities. There was no doubting this room's purpose, thought John. Despite the strangeness of the design of the equipment he immediately thought 'laboratory'.

'We use this area for research,' said the voice in his head as if confirming his suspicions.

'Have you any microscopes?' he found himself asking.

At this, a tall entity led him to a large unit with a centre console on top of which were square translucent panels. He then placed a glass phial, filled with liquid, on one of the panels, passed his hands over the unit and another square panel slid out over the top of the phial. A bluish glow filled the space between the panels.

At this moment an enlarged hologram of the phial appeared over the centre of the console. Angles and magnifications altered as the entity made adjustments by touching the top panel.

'This apparatus performs the same function as a microscope,' said the voice in John's head. 'But this one is far superior.'

John and his guides then moved out of the lab into a connecting tunnel and then into what the entities told him was a rest room.

Here four sets of couches, each slightly undulating and covered in a bubble-like material, were suspended one above the other. They were used for sleep periods and also for deep space travel for which each couch was equipped with its own mini-atmosphere, John was told.

Out again into the tunnels, through another room and up a vertical tube. John felt himself coming up through the floor into a large area. He immediately realised it must be the control room.

Four other tall entities were seated at a crescent-shaped unit which was covered in panes. Although they were facing away from him, John could see they were busy passing their hands over the unit before them, obviously fully occupied with controlling the craft.

John was ushered over to a couch on which he lay down. A dish-shaped object was placed a few inches above his head and as soon as he became settled pictures were projected onto the wall facing him. Short, sharp pictorial sequences, including maps and diagrams, flicked before his eyes at such a rapid pace that he could not take them all in. From the dish at his head came a garbled commentary.

'It's going too fast,' said John.

'Don't worry,' said the voice in his head. 'It is all being remembered by your mind.'

Star maps, cross-sections of the craft, scenes from the solar system flickered before him. *Phobos*, the name kept popping into his mind. *Phobos*.

He didn't discover until later that *Phobos* is the name of the smaller of the two moons of Mars.

After the bizarre picture show ended, the entities led John to a darker section of the control room where he was asked to look in a certain direction. Instantly a hologram burst into life before his eyes.

He was looking at a planet, an alien planet. The closer the view, the stranger it seemed, yet John could make out metallic cone-like shapes, sprouting from the ground of this world in bizarre formation. Perhaps a city.

Behind the city he could see mountains. Bands of colour stretched across the sky. The atmosphere seemed dense.

'This is what our own planet looked like in its last years,' said the voice in John's head. 'Ruined by pollution and natural problems . . .'

A figure appeared in the foreground of the hologram, dressed in a hooded robe. It was holding onto a glowing object with both hands. The round object glowed red and yellow. John was asked to touch it, which he did. As his finger made contact with the object a strange tingling sensation swept up his arm.

Overwhelmed by a feeling of having been honoured, as if he had been given the chance to glimpse the holiest of holy shrines, he tried to grasp what his hosts were trying to tell him.

'It is time to go,' said the voice in his head. 'We will meet again.'

With a sudden judder, John was back behind the wheel of his moving car.

After seeing John led away from the balcony and after her forced separation from Kevin, Sue was filled with a sense of dread. The examination room she was led to contained two tables, one slightly concave and one flat. Behind them were arranged an array of instruments, leads and boxes.

Frightened and struggling, she was somehow lifted onto one of the tables. Straps were drawn across her arms and legs, tightened and she was unable to move.

Looking around her in a wild panic, she saw two of the 'ugly' creatures whose description matched exactly the two who examined her husband.

They set to work immediately, drawing a pen-like, glowing instrument across the whole of her body. Starting at her feet, the pen thing was moved slowly up her body to her head. The examiners seemed to enjoy their work, thought Sue as she listened to the humming, almost singing sounds coming from the pair.

Frightened and continuing with her vain struggle, Sue

watched as one of the tall entities drew close. The examiner nearest to her immediately moved to make way for his obvious superior.

'We cannot do anything with you while you are like this,' chided a voice in Sue's head. The tall entity looked down and placed the middle finger of his right hand on her forehead, the two outer fingers on her eyes.

Sue blacked out.

When she came round she was still on the table, but the straps had been removed. Still she could not move.

One of the tall beings came into view and Sue immediately knew she could leave the room.

When she was placed upon the table she could not recall having any clothes on, but now as she climbed off she saw she was wearing a long gown with a tight hood, similar to that worn by the aliens. The baggy sleeves were brought in at the cuffs. The material was opaque, but looked like crinkly cellophane.

Like John, Sue was then taken on walk-about by two of the tall beings. The first thing she noticed was that all the walls of the craft were covered by a honeycomb structure.

At one point on her journey she recalls seeing John in his one piece suit, moving in the opposite direction, accompanied by two entities. Neither acknowledged the other, apparently more engrossed in the wonders around them.

Sue then arrived in the craft's control room. Like her husband she found herself ascending into the large chamber and immediately guessed its purpose from the lay out and from the level of activity.

One of the tall entities, seated in a chair, swivelled around to face her and took hold of her hand. As he helped her climb the step up to his level the words: 'That wasn't so bad, was it?' formed in her brain. She knew he was communicating by telepathy.

Still uneasy, Sue sat in a moulded seat indicated by the alien. She felt as if she were floating as she glanced about the large room, noting the units and control panels.

A tray containing about a dozen pink discs was offered to her. She thought the discs looked like pink peppermint creams. They were obviously some kind of food.

'I'm not going to take one, they could be drugged,' she thought. The beings either read her mind or understood her apprehension. They removed the tray immediately.

The entity who was seated – Sue automatically thought of him as the leader – looked at one of those standing. Sue seemed to understand that he had been given an order.

The standing entity then began slowly moving his hands, his fingers tracing strange shapes in the air. Immediately the room was filled with strange harp-like sounds.

Somehow Sue knew that the soft strains that drifted through the air from the direction of the standing entity were meant to be relaxing. But she was still tense with fear and with concern for her husband and children.

The leader seemed to understand.

'Your children are safe.' Again the words entered her mind. 'You value your children. We do not reproduce. We do not have children. We produce through you. You are our children.'

Now Sue felt relaxed. The message was reassuring and now the music seemed to be having an effect.

She looked over at the standing alien as his hands danced through the air. 'Everyone has a talent,' came the leader's telepathic message. 'This is a music man. This is his talent.'

When the music stopped, Sue was ushered over to another seat nearer to the controls. Pointing at an array of squares the Leader ran through the operating procedure. Touch this one and the craft will do that; touch this and it will bank.

The Leader turned away to communicate with one of his colleagues, then turned back to Sue and asked: 'Would you like to see where you live?'

'Yes,' she cried excitedly. A rectangular screen materialised to her right. The scene was a mass of stars. The entity pointed to a tiny pinpoint of light in the bottom right hand corner.

'Here is where you live,' came the words. The star grew larger until it became obvious it was the sun. Then the planet earth came into view, closer and closer until Europe and then Great Britain filled the screen.

Then the Thames Estuary came into view, roads, streets

and street lights. It was Aveley in Essex. Sue could see her home, there was no doubt about it.

The screen went blank and Sue, stunned by the images, reeled as a feeling of intense homesickness passed over her. Whether those views of her home were real or not they made Sue wonder about John and the children. Where were they? Were they safe?

The Leader had said they were safe but she wanted her children now. She needed them, now.

Another of the tall beings interrupted her thoughts and led her to a darker area of the control room where he indicated she should lie down facing a screen above her head. Like John, she was shown a high-speed series of images accompanied by sounds. They seemed like old cinema newsreels and high speed TV documentaries.

'It was like having the contents of an encyclopaedia pumped into your head all in one go,' said Sue later.

Unlike her husband, Sue has a clear memory of only one piece of information imparted by the strange audio-visual show, a chart of our solar system.

She remembers being confused about the planetary scene. There was the sun, there was Saturn with its rings and the massive Jupiter.

She counted the planets that ringed the sun, and counted them again. There was no doubt about it, there were ELEVEN worlds whirling around the star Sol instead of the nine known to conventional knowledge.

The screen above Sue's head went blank and an entity helped her up from the couch and led her silently down a slope into what she describes as a black area.

John and Kevin were standing there when a hologram materialised before them. She saw the scene that had confronted John – the alien's home planet and the hooded figure – and she distinctly remembers an explanation of sorts forming in her mind.

'This is the seed of life, our past and your future, our whole existence,' as before the words simply formed in her mind. 'Accept this from us for yourself, your children and your fellow man.'

As John and Kevin gazed at the figure holding the glowing

orb, or ball, Sue recalls the command: 'Touch the ball, touch the ball,' filling her mind. John and Kevin were already reaching out to the figure in the hologram. Their hands were making contact with the glowing orb. Slowly, Sue stepped forward and faced the figure who held the object.

The compelling urge to make contact overcame her and inch by inch she raised her right arm, reaching forward until she touched it. No feeling, no sensation, but as Sue turned away from the hologram more words were forming in her brain: 'It is time to go, but we will see you again.'

In the blink of an eye Sue's surroundings changed dramatically.

It was misty and vague and she was getting dressed. 'Are you dressed yet, John ?' she asked. 'Give Kevin a hand,' she added.

John said Kevin was already dressed.

'We'd better get a move on then,' said Sue as she took a large gulp from a glass that was not a glass, some kind of drinking vessel. As she set the cup down the scene changed again.

Now she was standing on a catwalk looking down on the family car about six feet below. Steps led down to the vehicle which was parked facing downwards on a sharply sloping ramp. In front of it was a horseshoe-shaped wall.

The Leader was standing by Sue and they were joined by the Music Maker whom the Leader addressed as Ceres. The Music Man now addressed the Leader as Lyra. The goodbyes that were forming inside her head were from the entities, of that Sue was sure.

Looking down she saw John climb into the car, the children were already in, and then slowly the vehicle began to dematerialise.

'It just seemed to "fizzle" out of existence,' recalled Sue later as she described how the car seemed to pass through 'the horseshoe-shaped wall, front bumper and bonnet first.'

The whole area became very bright as the car silently passed through the wall until it eventually disappeared.

Concerned, Sue looked forlornly at the Leader. 'Don't worry, you are going home,' he said.

When she next looked down she saw the white Vauxhall Victor as it bowled along the country lane by the woods. She remembers effortlessly climbing into the moving car and closing the door behind her.

She noticed the interior light was on, then a jolt.

'Is everybody here?' she remembers asking as she found herself beside her husband in the family car. John's reassuring 'yes, of course' was enough to quell the sense of panic that threatened to engulf her.

John and Sue Day's Close Encounter of the Fourth Kind is probably one of the most complete records of such a case in the UK. Exhaustively investigated their account remains unchanged to this day.

One of the most unusual aspects of this case is the sheer volume of information gleaned from their abductors.

Whether this detail was imparted telepathically or by some other means they do not know. Much of the information was volunteered by John while in a hypnotic trance. Other material came from John and Sue much later. The recalling of one or other fact during the regression seemed to bring back a further rush of forgotten detail.

John believes the beings told him that human evolution was only a part of the jigsaw of our development. The earth, he claimed, had been seeded by alien watchers for thousands of years. Seeding appeared to involve interbreeding.

But they also had the power to alter minds and physical structures to help the species become more aware and intelligent.

John said the Watchers, as he called them, had many contacts on earth. They could live for an indefinite period of time, but when their 'shells' ceased to function they had to move on to a new 'host'.

They also allegedly confirmed that they were the 'Gods' of Greek mythology. At that time they were more involved in the affairs of our planet. But they greatly reduced their level of involvement when they discovered it was leading to stagnation of human society.

Human development slowed down when denied control of its own destiny. They pulled back despite the fear that we could develop into a very violent and destructive life form, said John.

Did this mass of information really come from alien beings who abducted the Day family less than twenty miles from the City of London? Or was it a case of group hysteria – but on a smaller scale.

Contamination does not apply. The Days' knowledge of the subject was minimal.

The couple did not seek publicity or notoriety. They contacted Ufologists in a desperate attempt to discover more about their experience. They had absolutely nothing to gain by 'coming out'.

They even provided detailed drawings and diagrams of what they believed they had seen.

Investigator Andy Collins was impressed with the family. But he was astounded at the way John, a working class Cockney, could speak articulately and without interruption about the most complex subjects for up to twenty minutes.

'I just switched on the tape and let him speak,' said Andy who was then able to transcribe the tape to text verbatim, confident that it would always be in good, clear English.

If he asked John, a poorly educated man, to repeat aspects of the material he had dictated, he couldn't. In fact on one occasion, when told that he had been speaking authoritatively for fifteen or twenty minutes on a particular subject, John could not believe it.

'It was as if someone had switched on a tape inside him,' recalled Andy.

Did whoever it was who switched on that tape, also programme it with the abduction story he related? Cynics might find the reiteration of the Greek mythology/aliens line a little hard to swallow.

They might also wonder why it took this family so long to realise what a treasure trove of information they had been bequeathed by their abductors.

THE ULTIMATE ENCOUNTER

The British UFO researchers who have long argued that close encounter experiences are totally subjective and due to some kind of psychological or physiological process will rarely be moved even in the face of a multiple witnessing of an abduction.

Psychologists can always come up with psychological reasons for multiple events.

The possible rational causes for these events are many and largely based on hallucination.

So it does not matter how credible the witnesses, how detailed their account or how real their experience. The school of thought which favours a psychological approach to Ufology will not question the truth of the witnesses' testimony, or its reality. They will question their perception of reality.

It's a heads I win, tails you lose philosophy based on the premise that flying saucers and aliens don't exist.

If the alleged abductee is not a fake, then there is something askew in the mind.

So pity the poor investigator relying on the single abductee. His whole case is based on one individual's account of events. Back up might come from a good hypnosis session, but even that evidence is questionable.

He would count himself lucky to find additional evidence: marks on the ground to support claims of a UFO landing, marks on the body of the abductee to support claims of physical and medical testing, and a witness of impeccable character and credibility would make for a cast-iron case in Ufology terms. However, in the real world, none of the above is sufficient proof of UFOs, aliens or alien abduction.

Let's face it, the serious hoaxer can fake the story, fake the marks and put on an Oscar-winning performance under hypnosis if he really wants to.

So how does an investigator get sufficient proof to support the close encounter he is probing?

Well, no investigator is ever likely to get enough proof to satisfy every cynic. They just have to live in hope that the next case is the BIG ONE.

Peter Hough, chairman of the Manchester UFO Research Association, was convinced he'd got the big one a few years ago. The case that fell into his lap had all the right elements.

A former Metropolitan police officer, a UFO, an alien entity sighting, a clear case of missing time ... and a PHOTOGRAPH.

Yes, a photograph of an alien, a little green man. And it had been taken by a former policeman. What more could one want?

Peter could not believe his luck when the witness, after being subjected to hours of interviews, further agreed to undergo hypnotic regression in an attempt to discover more about his particular encounter.

That session was also a success and this Close Encounter of the Fourth Kind has now become a classic case, one that has gone down in the UFO history books.

Fellow investigators Arthur Tomlinson and Jenny Randles were also deeply involved in the case that was billed 'The Ultimate Encounter'.

The witness had shunned all suggestions of publicity on the grounds that he wished to return to the police force, but agreed to hand over the photographic evidence for expert testing.

He was the perfect close encounter witness: intelligent, co-operative and uninterested in making any financial gain from his experience.

Surely this was the case that would wake up the world to the reality of alien abduction. A British bobby photographs the alien who space-napped him and lives to tell the tale.

Sadly the world outside the confines of Ufology didn't bat an eyelid when the story was released.

The picture hadn't been faked, but the alien seen in it could have been a dummy. The policeman told his story, but no one wanted to listen.

For investigator Peter Hough it had been quite a trial.

Philip Spencer (pseudonym),
1 December 1987,
Ilkley Moor,
West Yorkshire.

The sun still hadn't risen when former police constable Philip Spencer set off from his home to cross the bleak moor over Ilkley, on a dull, dark winter's morning.

A quick glance at his watch told him it was 7.15 a.m. He checked he had his compass and his camera and then trudged off in the direction of East Morton, the village where his father-in-law lived.

A methodical man Philip had already decided his route across Yorkshire's most famous moor. Instead of taking the tourist trek from East Morton, he would take the shorter, but much tougher, alternative up a steep hillside.

Even though he had made the five mile journey many times, Philip always took his compass along. He knew how easy it was to become disorientated up on the cold and misty moor. Even the most experienced walker could get lost up there when the weather turned.

When the rain came down like stair-rods, as it often did, you couldn't see your hands in front of your face. And in the depths of winter, a sudden heavy snowfall could turn the moor into a white wasteland, obliterating every landmark as far as the eye could see.

Still there was no sight more grand than the view over Ilkley, seen from high up on the moor. And if the light improved he could get some good snaps of the town later, thought Philip, patting the pocket containing the camera that had served him so well for years.

A stiff wind began building up as Philip got stuck into the task of scaling the steep, grass covered hillside. Despite maintaining a steady pace he could still feel the biting cold through his sturdy hiking gear.

Careful to avoid rabbit holes and patches of slippery lichen, Philip made good progress. As the hill began to level out he spotted a path which ran alongside a row of trees.

Heading for the firmer footing of the track he was suddenly aware of a humming sound coming from above. He glanced at the lowering sky, assuming the mass of clouds was hiding an aircraft.

Then something caught his eye. Philip stopped and turned, peering into a large hollow, scooped out of the top of the hill. There, about thirty feet away, he saw what he later described as a 'small green creature'.

'Hey,' shouted Philip, as it scuttled off over the heather. It certainly wasn't human though it had a head, two legs and two long arms. The thing stopped when it was about fifty feet away, turned and waved.

With instinctive coolness, Philip reached into his pocket, pulled out his camera, brought it to eye-level and clicked the shutter.

Then, shoving the camera back in his pocket, he jumped down the embankment and gave chase.

'I don't know why,' he said later. 'But I just ran after it.'

Philip's running was reduced to a stumbling over the rough terrain, but when he saw his pursuer the creature darted around a huge outcrop and disappeared.

Using his hands to maintain his balance, Philip made his precarious way around the outcrop as quickly as he could.

Breathless and now sweating from his efforts, despite the cold, he worked his way around the mass of rock to find himself looking down into an even deeper hollow in the side of the hill.

The sight that met him nearly sent him careering back down the slope.

There, sitting at the base of the hollow was a strange object that almost defied description. The down-to-earth one time bobby saw what appeared to be two giant silver saucers, apparently stuck together edge to edge. A box shape protruded from the centre of the top saucer and was slowly descending into the object.

Philip found it impossible to gauge its dimensions from his vantage point, but the humming noise he had heard earlier had returned and was gradually increasing in intensity.

As the sound continued it's almost deafening crescendo, the object shot straight into the clouds.

Shaken and confused Philip decided to cut short his journey

and slowly made his way back off the moor heading in the direction of Ilkley. His confusion became more acute as he walked into the town.

It was a hive of activity. Shops were open, pedestrians lined the streets and traffic was building up on roads that were normally quiet at this time of the day.

Philip looked up at the town hall clock . . . and then did a double take. There was no mistake. The clock said it was 10 a.m. Yet he estimated that it should have been no more than 8.15 a.m. Surely no more than an hour could have elapsed since he set off from home.

'Am I going mad?' he asked himself as he mentally re-traced his steps from his home, up on to the moor and on into Ilkley. Philip was a man whose police training had honed his powers of observation. Estimating times, distances and speeds are all a part of the daily routine of a police officer so how was it he had 'lost' one and three quarter hours?

Then he remembered the photo. He knew a place in the nearby town of Keighley which operated a one hour photo-graphic developing service.

He caught the next bus to the town and walked to the shop, taking a couple of pictures as he went. 'I had felt guilty about wasting so much film,' Philip recalled later.

He handed in his roll of film and then walked around the town to fill in time. His mind went over and over his route on the moor, searching for rational explanations for the missing time. But there were none.

'What if the picture shows nothing?' he said to himself. That would mean he had no evidence of something strange up on the moor . . . maybe that would prove that he was indeed going mad.

When he returned to the shop he collected the prints nervously and marched straight into the street where he began tearing open the package and riffling through the contents, desperate to find the picture that would show he wasn't crazy.

There it was. The quality was poor, but there was no doubt about it. He had captured on film the thing he had seen with his own eyes.

That night, back at home, Philip went over the events of the day for the umpteenth time. The familiar walk to the moor, the slow ascent up the hillside, the encounter with the strange green creature. Yes the light had been poor and the creature had been green, a darker green than the grassy background. But there was no doubt about it. He had seen it.

He still didn't know why he had given chase. It had been a sudden impulse. A hunter in pursuit of his quarry doesn't think before closing in. He had not thought before acting. Thank God he had taken that photograph first. If it hadn't been for that fuzzy colour print he would now be doubting his own sanity.

In bed later that night Philip tossed and turned. Flashes of the green creature and the strange craft kept sleep at bay. The questions kept coming. What was it? Where had it come from? Did it go into the saucer object? How could it have risen into the sky so rapidly?

Bleary-eyed after a fitful night Philip sat down to breakfast the next morning feeling a growing sense of determination. He was not mad, he had not imagined events, he had seen something very strange on Ilkley Moor. Today he would go to the public library and look for some agency or organisation which could help him. He had heard of UFOs and all that nonsense. There must be someone out there who would be interested in hearing his story.

The letter from Philip that landed on the desk of UFO researcher Jenny Randles related his account in a matter-of-fact way. He briefly mentioned the photograph and pointed out that the compass he had carried that day was now totally useless. Its readings were inaccurate.

Because of his former links with the police force and his desire to rejoin the service Philip was very wary of attracting any publicity that might affect his chances of donning his uniform in the future. So instead of giving his address, the letter simply carried a PO Box number in Bristol, the city where his parents lived.

Jenny raised the case with the Manchester UFO Research Association where the reaction was restrained. They had received many letters over the years containing the most astounding claims, most of which could not be supported with evidence. Jenny was encouraged however to reply and ask for further details.

Meanwhile Philip was already regretting his clandestine approach. He simply wanted to report the matter to people who investigated such things and he wanted them to get to work now. He was desperate for someone else to confirm he wasn't mad and was not suffering from hallucinations.

He also needed to know that other people had experienced similarly disturbing events.

Even his wife Susan was having difficulty reconciling his story with his normally down-to-earth, no-nonsense nature. It was all just too fantastic to be true, she thought, and that's what everybody would think even if they didn't say it, wouldn't they?

The sheer strangeness of his experience was infuriating for Philip, a man used to confronting problems and solving them.

Losing patience, Philip decided to telephone another name that he had dug up in his researches at the library. Arthur Tomlinson, a man who had studied UFOs for thirty years, took the call at the end of December.

Accompanied by flying saucer enthusiast Steve Balon, Arthur, who was also a leading light in the Manchester UFO group, immediately travelled to Ilkley to meet Philip and together the three men re-traced his steps to study the location.

Philip had no qualms about handing over the photographic print and the negatives for testing. In fact, he was heartened by the enthusiasm displayed by Arthur and Steve. They had listened with interest and indicated similarities between what he had seen and other incidents. They did not question his sanity, which was heart-warming to him to say the least.

In the following days Arthur liaised with Peter Hough, chairman of the Manchester UFO Research Association. He pointed out that, in addition to the photograph, Philip had a further piece of evidence, his compass.

Arthur had studied the instrument and decided it had reversed its polarity, pointing south instead of north.

Peter agreed to join Philip, Arthur and Steve on a further expedition to the site on 3 January 1988.

Before setting off for the moor, the party met at Philip's home where Peter expressed some disappointment with the quality of the picture. It was grainy and lacking in detail. However he agreed that the entity appeared to have a long body, short legs and protuberances at the side of the head which could have been large ears.

The thin arms were long, the left one exceedingly so, because it appeared to be resting on the ground.

Philip recounted his story once again. It had not changed in any way since he first told it. Nevertheless, investigator Peter Hough was unhappy at Philip's laid back attitude in view of the traumatic nature of such incidents.

He felt Philip was treating the entire affair with a degree of amusement. Was he making it up, had he built a dummy, taken it onto the moor and photographed it?

He decided to put those thoughts bluntly to the witness to test his reaction. If he didn't voice reservations now, someone else would when the story was eventually made public.

Philip reacted instantly. Quite calmly he said: 'I am not particularly interested in what other people think. I know what I saw and if people don't believe me that's up to them.

'I've got nothing to gain by doing that (faking the picture). I don't see the sense, I've got better things to do with my time.'

The investigators knew, in fact, that Philip had a great deal to lose by coming forward with his account. A police force would be loathe to take on a constable with a history of flying saucer spotting, much less a hoaxer.

As the four men made their way to the site, the swirling storm clouds and biting winds of Wuthering Heights country added a touch of irony. How odd that this bleak landscape which had spawned such a classic of literature might also be responsible for an entirely new chapter in the history books of Ufology.

After a twenty minute walk from their cars, the men reached the spot where Philip had taken his photograph. The distance from the camera to the approximate spot where the small figure had been seen standing measured thirty nine feet.

The terrain was much as Philip had described it. There were no markings in the depression where he had seen the strange object and no other clues at the site.

The men made their way back, a heavy storm was imminent. The investigation now centred on the photograph.

The camera was a 35mm Dixons' own brand called a PRINZ Mastermatic, a basic lightweight model, constructed largely of plastic, with a 45mm lens. An internal light meter had not worked for some years.

According to Philip the camera had been pre-set for low light conditions, and loaded with the 400 ASA film. It should have taken a good picture. The dark and grainy picture it produced was interesting. It should have been slightly over exposed rather than underexposed.

The investigators spotted another anomaly in the picture. Although Philip estimated he took the photo around 7.45 a.m., the sky above the horizon in the picture was light when it should have been dark at that time on the 1st of December.

Extensive testing of the photograph by individual photographers, experts and Kodak in the UK came up with disappointingly inconclusive results.

All agreed that the picture was NOT a photograph of a photograph and the film had not been tampered with AFTER processing.

The figure, whatever it was, was actually there at the site when photographed.

Meanwhile the University of Manchester Institute of Science and Technology devoted some of their substantial technical know-how to the mystery of the compass and its reversed polarity.

After some days' tests in the lab, the university's Total Technology Department came back. Yes, it was possible to reverse the polarity of the compass without expensive and complicated equipment.

Simply take a piece of wire, coil it, place the compass inside the coil and connect to the mains electricity supply. Switch on and the polarity is reversed.

The process would be accompanied by a very loud bang and some blown fuses, said the expert, but it could be done, albeit with a certain risk to life, limb and property.

Would Philip Spencer have known how to conduct such a potentially dangerous experiment when an expert in the field did not immediately know how to do so?

While these various tests were being carried out, Philip Spencer had a more down to earth problem.

On Friday 15th January 1988 an angry Philip phoned investigator Peter Hough: 'What do you know about two men from the Ministry of Defence who've just been to see me,' demanded the normally quietly spoken man.

'They have shown me their identity cards with their names on and they said they wanted to interview me about my UFO experience.'

Peter assured Philip that his case was still entirely confidential and that no information had been passed onto anybody, including the MOD.

According to Philip two business-suited men identifying themselves as David Jefferson and Mr Davies had called at the house.

Reluctantly, he had given them a brief run down of his experience without mentioning the photograph. But they specifically asked about photographic evidence, and when Philip admitted taking a snap they asked to examine it. Philip told them it was with a friend, at which both men left.

'I'm worried that this situation is getting out of hand,' Philip told Peter. 'What if the media get hold of the story? What if my picture gets lost? I'll have no proof of what happened.'

Peter tried to reassure Philip and then immediately wrote to the MOD about the alleged visit. He never received a reply.

The following day Peter received another call from Philip. This time a national newspaper wanted to ask him about his UFO incident.

The former policeman had been adamant on no publicity. He was now withdrawing all co-operation and demanded the return of the picture and his compass.

Efforts to track down the reporter failed, but there were no press follow ups and Philip, after a great deal of persuasion, reluctantly agreed to allow the investigation to continue.

His reaction to the possibility of publicity reinforced the view of the investigators that Philip was not a hoaxer. He had no motive. He had no interest in selling his story, or his picture, he valued his anonymity and was determined to resume a police career.

When the results of the tests on the photograph and the compass came in, Philip was as disappointed as the investigators.

He had hoped that scientific examination would have found something that would have thrown some light on his missing one and three quarter hours, or would have helped provide some explanation for the green creature and the saucer-like object.

The subject of hypnosis was broached. The investigators thought Philip would be a good case for hypnotic regression and explained that it was a process where the subject is regressed to the time of the incident in the hope that he can recall events that occurred during his lost time. Philip agreed to try the technique. After all, he had nothing to lose.

On 6 March1988, Dr Jim Singleton, a consultant psychologist with no particular interest in UFO phenomenon, met Philip and agreed to regress him. The doctor insisted that none of the investigators be present during the session but agreed to an independent witness 'sitting in' to operate the tape recorders.

Once in a trance-state Philip was told to cast his mind back and re-experience the events of that bleak December morning.

The following account is taken from a verbatim transcript of the tape recordings made during the hypnosis session.

> Philip: I'm walking along the moor. It's quite windy and there are a lot of clouds. Walking up to the trees. I can see this little something, can't tell, but he's green. Moving towards me. Oh. I can't move. I'm stuck. He's still coming towards me. I still can't move ... I'm stuck and everything's gone fuzzy. I'm ... I'm floating along in the air. I want to get down. And this green thing is walking ahead of me and I don't like it. I still can't move. I'm going round the corner and this green thing's in front of me. Oh God ... want to get down.

> After a long pause Philip continued, his breathing much faster than before.

> Philip: There's a ... there's a big silver saucer thing, and

there's a door in it. I don't want to go in there . . . Everything's gone black now.

Dr Singleton: You say its gone black?

Philip: Mmmm. I can't see anything, like I'm asleep. Can't hear anything . . . Now there's a bright light, can't see where it's coming from. I'm in a funny sort of room. I can hear this voice saying don't be afraid. I don't feel afraid anymore. I can still see this green thing but I'm not frightened of it now . . .

Philip: I'm being put onto a table. I can move now if I want to but I don't feel frightened. And there is a beam-like pole. It's above me. It's moving up towards me. It's got a light in it. Like a fluorescent tube. It's coming up from my feet. I can hear that voice again, saying we don't mean to harm you and don't be afraid. Makes me feel warm as it's moving up me. It's coming up over my stomach, towards my head. Close my eyes, I don't want to look at it in case it hurts my eyes. It's gone . . . . There's something . . . My nose feels uncomfortable.

At this Philip wrinkles his nose.

Philip: That's gone as well. I'm standing up now, I don't know how I got stood up. I can see a door. There's one of these green creatures motioning for me to come with him. Don't really want to go with him. I'd rather stay in here. I don't feel afraid in here.

(After a long pause Philip continued)

Philip: I'm walking towards the door. There's still a bright light. I can't see where it's coming from. There's light all around. Want to know where the light is. It's just bright, it's just light. Walking down a corridor. There's a hole opened in it so I can walk through. I'm in a big room, a big round room, I'm on a raised platform against the wall. My camera and my compass are trying to get away from me, going towards the ball. It's difficult to pull them back down again and this ball's moving around, with things around it. Looks strange. It's got some blocks on it. He says we can't stay in here long. He wants us to go out again. The hole's closed in the wall. It's gone strange. He says I've got nothing to fear, but I'd like to go home . . . it's got such big hands.

(long pause)

Dr Singleton: What's happening now?

Philip: Going down a corridor again. It's very bright still. I wish I knew where the light was coming from, and there's another door. Going through a door: it's an empty room. Two of those green creatures have come with me. There's a picture. It's starting to move on the wall. Wonder how they get the pictures?

Dr Singleton: Pictures on the wall?

Philip: Mmm. Creatures seem concerned at the damage that it's doing. Pictures changing now, there's another picture, another film. He's asking me a question. He says do you understand? I said yes. It's time to go. Everything has gone black. I'm walking up near some trees. Some movement. I can see something, a green creature. I've shouted to it. It's turned round. I don't know what it is. I'll photograph it. It's turned round now.

Philip went on to describe his encounter with the saucer-shaped object before his walk in Ilkley. Still under hypnosis, he described the creature as about four feet tall. Detailed examination of the photograph indicated it's height as between four feet and four feet six inches.

He said it had large pointed ears, big dark eyes, no nose and a tiny mouth. The hands were very large with three large fingers like 'big sausages'. Its feet were V-shaped with two large toe-like digits and it appeared to have difficulty walking. 'He shuffles rather than walks,' explained Philip.

Of the two pictures, or films, he saw while on the craft Philip said the first involved scenes of destruction and starvation. But he refused to discuss the second saying only: 'I'm not supposed to tell anybody about the other film. It's not for them to know.'

Philip's description of events matched the classic elements of abduction experience: small creatures, couch in the centre of a room, physical examination, lights with no obvious source and ecological warnings, all matched similar accounts from around the world.

But was Philip really under hypnosis?

'Definitely,' said Dr Singleton. 'That's my opinion. To have faked it convincingly, Philip would have had to have studied hours of videotaped sessions. Then he would have to be a very good actor to carry it off.

'I think the hypnosis was genuine. He was certainly recounting the incident as something which had actually happened. He described things typically as someone would recall a past event. He compares very well with other non-UFO subjects.'

However the doctor added: 'Experimental studies suggest that people can modify, or vary their recall. So obviously there is no certainty that what is recalled under hypnosis is a hundred per cent. However, here I think I've helped Philip to recover memories that were hidden more deeply in his mind.'

Why were those memories hidden?

'In terms of my clinical work, if people experience things which are unusual, traumatic or frightening, the mind protects itself by pushing them deep into the subconscious. Hypnosis seems to lower the threshold of this barrier.'

Philip had been allowed to retain full conscious recall of his hypnotic narrative and when asked after the session how vivid was his recollection he replied: 'It was very clear. I have no trouble remembering what I saw.'

Through hypnosis it seemed clear that Philip had taken his photograph at the end of his experience rather than much earlier. This explained the missing time and the lightness of the sky in the photograph.

When quizzed on his reference to a view through a window Philip explained: 'It was the sort of view astronauts have during space missions. I could see the Earth. It was very beautiful.'

Some weeks after the hypnosis experiment Peter Hough bumped into Philip. He had since applied to re-join the Police Force and had collected a character reference in the form of a letter from a serving police officer. He showed Peter the letter which spoke of Philip's good character and honesty.

Since that meeting Philip has been in touch with investigators to pass on further newly remembered details. This is not uncommon with abductees. Once their mental barrier has been broken down with hypnosis it is not unusual for additional details to be remembered at a later date.

Philip recalled: 'The creatures seemed part of a team. They weren't acting as individuals, but more like bees, as if they were doing what they were programmed to do.

'I had a feeling of goodness about them. I don't think they would harm anybody. I would go so far, in retrospect, to say I actually liked them.'

THE NEARLY FILES

One of the biggest files in the UFO investigators' office is for the 'Possible Abductions'. The nearly cases that don't contain enough detail to be put down as classic Close Encounters of the Fourth Kind, yet which have factors which seem to point in the right direction.

They are a million miles away from the graphically described cases that we have looked at so far. The witnesses, at least some, are perfectly credible but their recollections are sometimes confused and unclear.

'Maybe I dreamed it', is one way of explaining the fantastic images and events some find lodged in their brains. It's often easier to dismiss these monster memories as nightmares than try to trace their origins.

Brief snatches of events are all that some people's memories retain, as if their brain has already censored out the impossible. Being haunted by these flash-backs drives some to seek help from various therapists.

They seem instinctively to know that something strange has happened to them, but they can't put it into words.

Those who describe their encounter with perfect clarity, then say they have a vague notion of missing time, may or may not have had an abduction experience. They may not suffer from the dreams which for some provide clues as to what happened during those missing minutes. They may not respond to hypnosis.

Some simply don't want to delve into their minds for memories which were presumably locked away for good reason.

In these cases there is no way of knowing whether or not they were removed from their homes or familiar surroundings, whether they underwent the testing reported by others or whether they made contact with beings from elsewhere.

Nevertheless their experiences are well worth recording . . .

George and Amanda Phillips (pseudonyms),
30 August 1982,
Redcar,
Cleveland.

George and Amanda Phillips had put their baby daughter to bed. A couple of hours in front of the television later and it was time for them to turn in. But that late summer's night took a sudden turn into the extraordinary at exactly 1.20 a.m.

Amanda remembers looking at the clock as a piercing scream from the baby's room left her shaking with panic. That was no ordinary scream, she said to George, as they both scrambled out of bed and headed for their ten month old tot. She sounded frightened or as if she was in pain.

George arrived in his tiny daughter's bedroom first and scooped her up into his arms. Amanda was close behind. She checked her child was physically alright before cradling the baby, Sarah, in her arms, a sense of relief washing over both of them.

At that moment both George and Amanda turned their heads towards the window. A bright, blinding light shone into the room from something in their back garden.

As they approached the window, George thought he could make out something, an object in the back.

'I had made the base for a shed and I could see something on the base,' recalled George later. 'It was oval in shape. And there was someone or something standing next to it.'

Shocked, he told Amanda to take a look at it and then headed out onto the landing. Something made him look over the bannister to the bottom of the stairs. Two small figures were making their way up.

'I don't remember anything after that,' said George during an interview with a UFO investigator some years later.

Relaxing at his semi-detached home in Redcar, Cleveland, the ICI factory worker seemed genuinely perplexed by the whole incident.

'It's so strange. I don't even remember waking up the next morning. The first thing I remember about the following day was opening up the door to the kitchen and saying to Amanda: 'I had a funny dream last night.'

'She said: "Well I had a funny dream as well." Then we both, more or less speaking at the same time, said, "an alien sort of thing".

'I asked her where she had seen it from and by this time Amanda was saying "Oh My God" as if the remembering was frightening her. Then she said "from Sarah's window".'

The couple went up to the child's bedroom to look for clues, only finding a damp patch on the floor by the cot.

'We were pretty sure it was urine, but it couldn't have been Sarah's because she was still in nappies. We assumed one of us must have wet ourselves that night from the fright.'

Some time later George took a tiny sample of liquid he had gathered up from the damp patch at the time and had it tested at the ICI plant where he was then working. An analyst friend did a pH test which confirmed it was indeed human urine.

Under questioning by a UFO investigator, George and Amanda realised their 'dreams' finished at different times. They both remember clearly being woken by their baby's screams and seeing the bright light at the window.

When pressed, George recalled the object in the backgarden as being small and oval with a ring of lights around it. He described what could have been three landing legs and antennae-like structures.

But his recollections stopped abruptly at the point when he left the child's bedroom to look over the landing at two creatures ascending the stairs.

During the interview Amanda took over the account at this stage.

She remembered following George out of the bedroom onto the landing. But when she got out there, there was no sign of George. He had disappeared completely.

She looked down the stairs and saw the creatures which had confronted her husband. Amanda described them as small, almost child-like in size, with pale skin, no hair or nose and no clothing that she could ascertain.

Both George and Amanda agreed to go under hypnosis to discover the truth about that strange night. But it was Amanda's account of events that suggest a possible abduction.

Once in a hypnotic trance, Amanda was taken back to moments before her baby's waking. Sarah's screams were the first thing she remembered, then the lights and then following George onto the landing.

> A: I had Sarah and I went on to the landing after George and he wasn't there. I didn't know where he was. I shouted 'George', but he didn't reply. Then there was a noise, someone downstairs. There's something on the stairs. Terrible . . . I don't know what it is.
> It's small, its skin is funny. It's like a child, pale, small, very small. Long face, very pale, no hair and I can't see any ears and I can't distinguish a nose. It's just standing there, still on the stairs. I see one behind, pale, I see two.
>
> Hypnotist: Are you still on the landing?
>
> A: The stairs appear
> H: So you are going downstairs?
> A: I can't see them any more, I can't see them.

(Amanda then says she feels as if she is going outside the house. Despite further questioning by the hypnotist, Amanda can't say where she is. She hasn't a clue about her location.)

> H: Where are you now?
> A: Outside
> H: Are you happy there?
> A: No.
> H: How do you feel?
> A: Frightened.
> H: Of what?
> A: I don't know where George is.
> H: Are you still outside the house?
> A: I don't know.
> H: How about Sarah, where's she?
> A: I don't know.
> H: What can you see?
> A: Nothing. There is . . . nothing.
> H: How light is it?
> A: Quite dark, I think. I'm not sure because I can't see anything.

H: Are you dreaming?

A: No, I'm not acting.

H: Where are you now?

A: Back in bed.

(Amanda then recalls waking up with her husband and discussing their dreams.)

Oddly, despite his graphic conscious account of the lights from the bedroom window and the creatures, George's version under hypnosis gave absolutely no indication of any unusual activity.

He described getting out of bed after being woken by his daughter's screams. Looking out of the window, he thought he saw a movement in the back garden, went to investigate, saw nothing and returned to bed.

George and Amanda Phillips, although disturbed by the events of that night, did not seek explanations immediately. They had no knowledge of, or particular interest in UFOs, and were content to carry on their lives as normal.

There were no after-effects that they could attribute to the lights or the creatures, no recurring dreams or flashbacks.

However George did become ill two months after the incident with a rare condition of the blood.

'It's a condition where your blood cells come under attack from your own immune system,' explained George. 'I was in hospital for about three months, couldn't walk, kidneys were being affected or something.

'Anyway, they treated me with steroids and it cleared up. The doctors said it was a condition that affected one in 100,000 people or something like that.

'Whether it had something to do with that night I don't know.'

It was sometime later that the couple were put in touch with a UFO research group. The couple had been intrigued by what sounded like a missing time incident, hence the hypnotic regression.

The Phillips are just another ordinary couple who experienced a very extraordinary night of events.

Although the investigators who studied the case could never prove it, they said that it definitely had the feel of an abduction.

Amanda's feeling of leaving the house and then the sense of fear and the inability to describe her surroundings begged the question: 'Where was she?'

Douglas Tams,
5 June 1974,
Stoke on Trent,
Staffordshire.

Douglas Tams was driving the last bus from Kidsgrove to Burslem Depot near Stoke on Trent on that warm summer's night. After a busy shift it was nice not to have any passengers to worry about. It was a quarter to one in the morning as he drove through Goldenhill.

There was very little traffic on the road at that time of night and Douglas was enjoying the starlit view of the valley that swept away to his left. As the draught from his open driver's window cooled him after the heat of a hectic day.

Suddenly the engine and all the lights in the vehicle cut out.

As the bus coasted to a halt Douglas looked down at the dashboard hoping a warning light might be flashing to indicate a fault, but it was in blackness. Just his luck to break down at the end of a shift, he thought. It would take the breakdown crew ages to get out here and God knows what time he'd get home. He couldn't very well catch a bus.

Wearily, he raised himself from the driver's seat, ready to climb out of the cab for a proper inspection of the bus. Suddenly he was forced to duck.

As he squeezed between his seat and the dashboard Douglas couldn't believe what he saw. A massive object seemed to be falling out of the sky and heading straight for his bus.

He counted the seconds until he was sure that the thing must have missed, otherwise he would have felt the impact by now.

Slowly pulling himself up, he steeled himself for another look through the windscreen. The thing was still there.

Ah, but now he could see that it hadn't really been on a collision course; it was now passing directly overhead.

'It's huge,' he said to himself as his eyes watched the three hundred feet wide oval-shape move slowly and with deliberation.

The giant mystery machine, for machine it obviously was,

followed an east–west flight path. It was difficult to estimate its height, but it couldn't have been very far above him, Douglas thought.

The underside of the object was illuminated by a green haze, less distinct than the bright ring of lights that defined its ovoid shape.

It probably took the UFO only a matter of two or three minutes to pass from one horizon to the other, finally disappearing from sight behind a line of houses, but to its sole witness it seemed an eternity.

'That's when the engine started and the lights came on, just like remote control,' said Douglas later.

He climbed into the driver seat, put it into gear and headed off on the ten minute journey to his depot, his mind going over the events of the last few minutes.

'When I got to the depot I was ONE HOUR late,' Douglas told a British UFO Research Association team. 'I did not say anything to my colleagues for fear of them taking the mickey and laughing at me.'

Despite being puzzled by the incident, especially the missing hour, Douglas declined the chance of becoming involved in a thorough investigation including possible hypnosis.

This down-to-earth, working class witness had no wish to 'dabble with the unknown', as he put it.

BUFORA investigators were disappointed by his reluctance to take the matter further. They felt there was a good chance that hypnosis would at least throw some light on his lost sixty minutes.

They hoped that in time, they could persuade Douglas to have a re-think and co-operate with a fresh investigation.

Sadly they didn't have the chance. Only a few years later, Douglas died, taking the mystery of that missing hour to the grave.

Abduction? This case had all the makings of such. A UFO sighting, engine and electrical malfunction and a full missing hour.

Douglas had no motive for fabricating the story. The missing hour had caused him problems at work. His bosses wanted to know why he was so late back at the depot. The problem with the engine and the lights were the only aspects he dared report to his superiors.

In fact he didn't reveal his full account to BUFORA investigators until fourteen years later.

James and Pam Millen,
6 September 1990,
Fleet,
Dorset.

Retired landscape gardener James Millen and his wife Pam were on a camping holiday at West Farm, near Fleet in Dorset, when they became contenders for the Ufologists' *could be* files.

James was fifty four at the time and he and Pam had driven down from their home in Putney, London, for a few days at the popular camp site which overlooks picturesque Chesil Beach.

West Farm campsite was less busy than usual. Peak camping season had just passed and the weather over the last few days had been a bit blowy, not ideal for living under canvas.

The couple had enjoyed a day's walking and retired to their large tent not long after darkness fell.

James takes up his story: 'I tend at my age to wake up in the middle of the night for the loo and that night was no exception. I made my way to the toilet block, which is in the same field, noting that there were only a few tents about, probably because of the weather.

'As I walked back, I gazed up at the stars. It was a clear night and I could make out the constellations beautifully. Over to the field on my left I could see an orange-golden glow — like sodium lamps. I thought the farmer must be working in the field, rounding up his cows for milking or something.

'Then I thought, that's funny. I hadn't noticed any poles in the field, so what had the farmer hung his sodium lamps on. I turned and looked again and there were several of these golden, orange balls of light, rising and falling in the sky.

'It was like someone was juggling with them. I stopped and tried to work out what they were. By now I was very close to our tent so I called for Pamela and she came out and watched them with me.

'I asked Pam what she thought they were and she just said "Don't ask me what they are, I don't know. Whatever they are they're doing something they shouldn't be doing."

'I remember saying to her that we were probably the only people in the south of England standing outside watching a display like this and at this time of night. I looked at my watch and it was five to three in the morning.

'Pam then said she was going back into the tent to make a cup of tea. I said I would watch the lights for a little while longer. Then I remembered my camera in the boot of my car and I thought I'll go and get my Praktica and get a picture of these things.'

At this point James' recall becomes hazy and disjointed.

'The next thing I remember is being back in the tent with Pam, telling her "they've gone now. If we don't get to bed we won't get any sleep at all tonight."

'Then Pam asked if I wanted a cup of tea and I said yes and then we sat down and just looked at each other without saying anything. It was if we were stuck in time somehow.

'Then Pam asked "What's that light coming through the tent?", so I looked out and I told her it was dawn. The sun was just coming up.

'Pam said: "That's early isn't it?", then we checked the time and it was 5.35 a.m.'

Somehow they had 'lost' more than two hours of their lives.

'I looked at my wife and she looked at me. We were astonished,' remembers James. 'Then I noticed cigarette ends, down by our feet.

'There were about eight of them and we were not in the habit of leaving cigarette ends on the floor. Pam said she had the distinct impression that she had been sitting there waiting for me, waiting for some time. She didn't know why, except that she just knew she had been sitting, waiting and smoking until I came into the tent.'

Tired and puzzled by their strange night, the couple decided to return home to London the next day. After packing up the tent and loading the car they agreed to make a detour so they could stop at Stonehenge in Wiltshire where James wanted to take some pictures of the ancient stones.

At the popular tourist site James took out his camera to find the lens covered in what he describes as a strange lime/mortar mixture.

'It was horrible stuff and difficult to remove,' he said. 'I couldn't understand where it had come from or whether it had any connection with the previous night's occurrence. I just chalked it up as another bizarre event.'

Although he has never been hypnotically regressed, James has experienced strange flash-backs about that night in Dorset.

' I have had mental pictures of my being in a strange room with lights on the walls, glowing lights. There is the impression of being surrounded by people, some tall, some short. I don't know how significant these dreams are but they are very odd.

'I can't explain any of this. I am not normally subject to illusions or hallucinations.'

Where did James Millen disappear to while his wife sat smoking nervously in their tent for more than two hours? Were the flash-backs of a strange room and strange people an indication of abduction?

His wife Pam had witnessed the lights which started off their experience, so we know they were not imagined, but sadly the missing time may always remain a mystery.

Investigators felt James would not be suitable for hypnosis due to his age and 'contamination', however they hope that in time he will find other pieces of the jigsaw falling into place, other memories surfacing that may give him a clue to his seaside encounter.

Maxine Watkins,
28 November 1988,
Holbury,
Hampshire.

Maxine Watkins was just twenty years old when she had an encounter with something more akin to the Hammer House of Horror than a UFO.

The youngster had just enjoyed an evening at her local working men's club and was walking home alone through the crisp November night. The time was approximately 11.20 p.m. and Maxine was probably no more than a couple of hundred yards away from home, and safety, when strange things began to happen.

As she turned into the avenue that would take her into the final stretch leading to her home she noticed the branches of the trees lining the road were waving furiously, as if in a gale.

But there was no wind, not even a gentle breeze.

Feeling frightened Maxine quickened her pace, anxious to get away from the spooky trees.

Suddenly a light appeared, a pulsating light. Maxine stopped and focused on the object she could see between the waving branches of the trees. It was round, or oval with lights, strong pulsating lights.

'Then it came right over me,' said Maxine later. 'This light shot out and then I was in this place . . . .'

She was in a strange room facing a man, a man with a bald head and wearing a flowing black cape with a high collar, 'a Dracula cape' was the way Maxine described it.

The Dracula figure was holding both his hands out-stretched, cupped in them was a ball or orb with a cross attached.

'I had this really intense fear,' said Maxine. 'The man with the ball was holding it up in front of him. There were another two beings there, one either side of him.'

Maxine then had the impression of movement which she found difficult to explain.

'I was moving, but not walking, like hovering, going along. I was taken to this table and they put me on it and clamped my legs so I couldn't move. The clamps were so tight they left marks which I could see the following day.

'I was being told something. It was like something in my head. I just shouted to them to let me go, let me go, but they wouldn't.'

'They were trying to reassure me but this had little effect.'

Maxine described the room in which she was in as oval 'like a conference room'.

As she was lying on what she assumes was an examination table, Maxine remembers her captors pulling down a complicated apparatus and placing it over her head.

'That was it, the next thing I knew I was down in the road and I had no idea how I got there.'

Maxine found herself in a crumpled heap on the pavement about a hundred yards down the road from the point where she had first seen the UFO.

'When I found myself on the ground, I looked up and the object just went *shisssh*. It shot up. It just disappeared in the sky.'

Maxine, now suffering from a severe headache and eye irritation, realised at this point that the whole sequence of events had been in total silence. The swishing of the object disappearing in the sky was the first noise she had been aware of since finding herself in the strange oval room.

Disturbed by her experience, Maxine wrote to the British UFO Research Association and an interview was arranged.

The circumstances of her experience, the lights and the removal to a strange place, have links with abduction phenomena, but the descriptions given by Maxine sound more like the set of a vampire B-movie.

The first being she saw was dressed like Dracula and he was holding a cross of sorts. Perhaps this was the only way she could describe a scene so removed from her normal experience.

Maxine did not undergo hypnosis, so her encounter joins those in the 'Possibles File'.

ANATOMY OF AN ABDUCTION

Are all abductions the same or do they differ widely? The reason this question is often posed is simple. If different people from different parts of the world report abductions which follow the same pattern this surely adds credibility to the theory that we are indeed the guinea pigs in an alien laboratory.

If the methods of capture, the details of examination and the mode of return are common then there is a greater chance of their being some truth in the experiences. If a selection of people from across the world make up such stories, how come they are so similar?

You would expect different folk from different backgrounds to imagine different tales.

Thomas E. Bullard, who holds a doctorate in folklore from Indiana University, researched and wrote a comparative study of alien abductions on behalf of the Fund for UFO Research in America, which looked at the question of the link between the phenomenon and folklore.

Dr Bullard's scientific examination of about three hundred abduction cases, most of them American, did not come up with any hard and fast conclusions on the abduction-folklore link. But it did offer a remarkable insight into the structure of abduction phenomena, breaking down a mass of abduction reports into their common denominators. Dr Bullard showed there was a sequential pattern of events in all abduction cases and many of the sequences he described in his paper can be identified in the British cases we highlight in this book.

From capture to return home, Dr Bullard identified each distinct stage of abduction experience and quantified their frequency in the mass of reports he studied. But this was not merely a statistical exercise, it was a serious attempt to find a satisfactory explanation as to why so many people were experiencing events which were so strange, yet so similar.

'The most remarkable thing about UFO abductions is that they happen at all,' states the doctor. 'The second most remarkable thing is that they happen so often. In quality and quantity, abductions best fulfil the meaning of the phrase: an embarrassment of riches.

'A striking but seldom noticed characteristic of abduction reports is the sequence of events that unfolds.'

Dr Bullard identified a maximum of seven stages through which abductees may pass. These include:

- capture
- conference (where the abductee converses with his captors)
- examination
- tour of the ship
- outworldly journey
- meeting with a divine or sacred being
- return and aftermath

'Not every case contains every episode,' explained the doctor. 'And some episodes are quite rare, but those that do appear follow this prescribed sequence. Out of one hundred and ninety three cases with two or more episodes, a hundred and sixty three show the correct order.

'Capture consists of four distinctive parts: intrusion, where a UFO appears and stalks the witness; zone of strangeness, where odd things seem to happen to the physical world; time lapse, where the witness suffers some form of mental impairment; and procurement, where the beings take the witness into custody.

'When two or more of these parts occur, they follow this order in seventy per cent of cases.

'Procurement has the complexity of a sub-episode in itself, with a sequence of eight recurrent events: a beam of light may strike the witness, a force may draw him, beings appear and a conversation follows.

'The beings pacify him or otherwise control the witness, they escort him to the ship and float him on board. He enters with a momentary loss of memory or doorway amnesia.

'Again seventy seven per cent of the cases with two or more of these events have the events arranged in the pre-scribed sequence.'

Dr Bullard also puts under his microscope the examination episode which many abductees report.

'The examination episode breaks down into eight distinct activities: the beings prepare the witness by undressing, cleaning and positioning the witness on a table. Then the actual examination moves from the general to more specific concerns as the beings first subject the witness to a manual exploration, apparently to gauge external characteristics,' says Dr Bullard.

'Next a scanning device, like an eye or light, passes over the witness, followed by instrumental investigations aimed perhaps at revealing internal structures and physiological functions.

'The beings then take specimens of skin, hair or body fluids and an examination of the reproductive areas comes next. At close examination, the beings show interest in the neurological system.

According to Dr Bullard a total of sixty nine per cent of the cases follow this pattern.

The way abductees report their return to the normal world also came under scrutiny in Dr Bullard's probe.

'The return episode begins with a farewell and thereafter reverses the capture,' he points out. 'The witness exits and experiences doorway amnesia once again as the beings float him outside.

'After watching the departure of the craft, the witness re-enters the normal world as he resumes his previous activities and memories of the abduction fade away. The four parts of this episode stay true to form in two thirds of the cases.'

Dr Bullard adds: 'What matters about the order of these events is that the pattern is not inevitable.

'A conference could follow the examination or specimen-taking, or the scan, and the change would make no difference to the story. It would still make sense one way or the other.

'The fact that witness after witness sticks to one arbitrary order suggests that the experience itself is structured that way.'

'The commonest prelude to the examination is a confer- ence, a more or less formal period of conversation between the witness and his captors.

'Four activities characterise the conference: the beings interrogate the witness about topics of interest to them; there is an explanation of where they come from and why they are here; they make a request of the witness, often to forget the experience, but sometimes to learn or improve himself, or bring them information at a future date; they warn that certain human behaviours are dangerous. Prophecies of coming events are also common.

'The prophecies usually predict coming disasters and even apocalyptic changes on Earth, events the aliens or an enlight- ened witness may mitigate. A few cases include a tour of the ship, apparently as a courtesy to the witness. This tour may include a glimpse of the engine room, where several wit- nesses report crystalline globes attached to a rotor device of sorts.'

Dr Bullard's researches also revealed that a number of witnesses experience an other-worldly journey to what some refer to as another planet. Witnesses often reported seeing bustling cities and ample signs of alien civilisation.

Rare is theophany, where the witness encounters a divine being or is introduced to something the beings regard as sacred in some way. After-effects from abduction include nightmares, eye irritation, sunburned skin and cuts or punc- ture wounds.

Long term changes may involve new interests, a desire for learning, the development of extra-sensory powers, a change of personality, sometimes for the better. Further encounters with aliens are not uncommon.

Paranormal experiences, visits by 'men in black', appari- tions and poltergeist-like phenomena may follow.

Interestingly, Dr Bullard points out: 'Not all consistencies in abduction stories are limited to the form and content of the episodes.

'The craft has a discoidal shape in a hundred and thirty six out of a hundred and sixty two cases. In some cases the disc is thick, in others thin, sometimes a dome or projections differentiate the craft, and sizes vary so much that witnesses compare the ship to anything from a small car to a football field.

'The craft are clearly not carbon copies, but a few cigar or other shapes challenge the general discoidal pattern.

'Once inside, the witness usually finds himself within a circular, domed room without sharp corners. Lighting is uniform and diffused without a specific source being visible. The atmosphere is usually cold and clammy and the air difficult to breathe because of its heaviness, or less frequently its noxiousness.

'The beings may be human, humanoid or monstrous,' he says. 'Humanoids make up two thirds of the two hundred and three cases where witnesses describe the beings, while humans appear in fifty two cases. The standard humanoid is of short to average height, has a large rounded head and enormous, compelling eyes. The nose and ears are small and even vestigial, while the mouth is no more than a hole or a slit. No hair grows on the grey, ashen skin, and the beings dress in tight overall uniforms.

'Some clues to the personality and the concerns of the beings emerge in abduction reports,' Dr Bullard's report finds. 'Most crews have a leader who converses with the witnesses, using telepathy to address the humans but a rapid, mumbling verbal speech to communicate with others of his own kind.

'The beings are polite in speech and behaviour, but their courtesy often proves false, a mere front to manipulate the witness and win his co-operation. In fact, the beings seem clinical and aloof, indifferent to and perhaps uncomprehending of human pain and fear.'

Dr Bullard's dissection of every detail from a mountain of abduction reports also found interest in reproduction and fertility to be a common denominator of many.

'The beings' interest in reproduction comes to the fore during the examination, but other hints reinforce the impression that matters of reproduction and fertility command a central place in their concern,' he says.

'In their conversations the beings may state outright that they have trouble reproducing, or a desire to reinvigorate their stock by combining with humans, or come from a dying, infertile planet. Observations of the otherworld confirm this admission.

'A preference for youthful captives is noticeable when a comparison of the ages of abductees is made. Also worth noting is that in two of the reports it seems that the beings rejected one witness for being too old and another because of a vasectomy.

'These choices make sense if interest in fertility is what motivates them. The tampering with the witnesses' genitalia and the scale of the abduction programme suggest beings in serious biological trouble exploiting human captives in an effort to survive.

'A number of strange phenomena are associated with abductions.

'Some effects apply to the physical world and others to the mind. Physical effects include a vacuum-like stillness surrounding the abduction site and influences on motor vehicles: some are the traditional electromagnetic effects familiar in UFO reports, while others are seemingly external control over the operation of the vehicle.

'The best known mental effect is time-lapse, a gap in the witness's memory during the period of abduction. The phenomenon appears in a hundred and sixty four cases, while other forms of mental impairment such as unconsciousness or lethargy boost the total even higher.

'The witness may behave in uncharacteristic ways while under the being's influence, and they seem to have a number of mind control techniques by which they pacify the witness, relieve pain and induce compliance with their wishes.

'Other effects lie in the shadowland between the physical and mental. The witness floats to the ship, but does he defy gravity or only feel as if he floats? Evidence points both ways. Cases of passing ghost-like through a solid wall and an isolation effect whereby the abduction takes place in an inhabited area in plain view, yet no one else intrudes, raise similar questions.'

Dr Bullard says the mountain of data he piled up for analysis provided only a molehill of conclusions.

'The ultimate nature of abduction eludes the study because

the real subject is not the experience itself but the abduction report,' he says.

The conclusion was that three explanations could account for the similarities among abduction reports:

The reports may be alike because different people share the same kind of objective experience.

The reports may be alike because different people share the same kind of subjective experience. This assumed some kind of universal psychological phenomenon capable of generating the mental images and feelings of abduction.

The reports may be alike because different people share the same story tradition. (Narrators then merely repeat the form and contents of stories heard from other narrators, or more plausibly a well-publicised report influences the perceptions and descriptions of subsequent witnesses so that they distort their own experience to conform to their expectations.)

Dr Bullard believes a case can be argued for each explanation but believes that his research has proved beyond a shadow of a doubt that 'abduction reports as a body show far more similarities than accident, random hoaxes or pure fantasies can explain'.

And he adds: 'The consistencies in form and content, down to numerous minute details, demonstrate that abductions make up a coherent phenomenon, whatever its ultimate nature. Any sceptic who dismisses this unity relies on hope rather than evidence to support his case.'

Dr Bullard's report was welcomed by abduction investigators and Ufologists who hope for other serious studies and further scientific research.

However, the branch of Ufology that argues that abduction experiences are simply a part of modern folklore will point to this work as supporting their contention.

Is our modern culture so steeped in UFOs, aliens and abductions that it becomes a handy explanation to pull out of the bag when rational explanations fail us?

True we are surrounded by a host of books, films and TV on UFOs and aliens. Yes, even a top US soap opera used an alien abduction plot as a bizarre yet entertaining audience puller.

But when confronted by strange and odd events are we really going to opt for alien abduction theory unless it fits the bill?

As we have seen from our cases so far, most are more specific than lights in the sky and missing time.

Folklore surely can't explain away Philip Spencer's experience. He saw a green creature, and photographed it. He saw a craft and much more if we accept what he related under hypnosis.

What about Robert Taylor? He saw a craft and two further objects. He detected an acrid smell; he heard the noise of the spiked spheres approaching him.

He *felt* those objects pulling at his clothing and then he and the police found the marks that indicated that something of several tons in weight had been sitting on the spot where he had seen the strange craft.

Robert Taylor had not used folklore to reconcile the irreconcilable. If he was having problems with his 'perception', what was the thing that he saw, heard, smelled and felt?

Dr Bullard's extremely thorough comparison of cases could not hope to come up with any real answers, but it was interesting to note how many of the abduction sequences found in American cases are also found here in our British casebook.

His work has, at the very least, presented an at-a-glance guide to the anatomy of an abduction.

VINTAGE VISITS

With not much more than a handful of years before the twenty first century and with the fiftieth birthday of the term *flying saucer* fast approaching, it is safe to say that the UFO, and Ufology, has come of age.

As we said in the last chapter, with our TV screens full of aliens, spacecraft, Star Trek and sci-fi shows galore, and with our cinemas packed with audiences hungry for ET and close encounters, today flying saucers are as much a part of our culture as fish and chips.

Ask any youngster what an alien is and he'll be spoilt for choice: Darth Vader, Mr Spock of the Starship Enterprise or ET — the cutest extra-terrestrial ever to come out of Hollywood.

So as a piece of modern day folklore alien abduction is not as outrageous as it at first seems. The terminology, the descriptions of the craft and the aliens are available in abundance if we wish to construct our own piece of abduction fantasy.

Although the abduction phenomenon, as we pointed out earlier in this book, goes back a long time, possibly thousands of years, those tales used a completely different terminology, a different vocabulary. Fiery chariots, not flying saucers, were ridden by angels or Gods, not aliens.

However the following reports come from a generation who were not at all familiar with the UFOs and flying saucers that we now take in our stride.

In those far off days before the information technology revolution the great British public got their daily diet of news from the papers, the Home Service and cinema newsreels.

The term *flying saucer* had only just been born, and would take a long time getting to these shores. The first alleged alien abduction had not yet been recorded. And the language of Ufology was unknown.

Yes, they may have had those early science fiction B

movies — H.G. Wells *War of the Worlds* was turned into a celluloid epic between the wars — and science fiction as a literary genre was beginning to make its mark in the States.

Dan Dare and Flash Gordon were beginning to appeal to the kids of the forties and fifties.

But ordinary folk in the years after the Second World War would not have a clue about abduction phenomena. UFOs and flying saucers would have seemed absolutely ludicrous . . . as ludicrous as spaceflight and man landing on the moon.

So how do we explain the very descriptive cases which we have on record from way back then? We can't accuse them of being contaminated, can we?

That all the reports that follow are from senior citizens whose encounters took place either during or shortly after the last war gives them added credibility.

Like the rest of the interviews in this volume, the witnesses have nothing to gain by recounting these events; they sought no reward. All three of the witnesses whose stories we recount had no knowledge of the subject at the time of their experiences, but in the years that followed developed a keen interest in UFOs and abductions. Because of the many years that have elapsed since their experiences, and the age of the witnesses, the detail is sometimes lacking. Memories may fade with the passing of time, but investigators still maintain that the ring of truth can be clearly heard across the decades.

Commander Horatio Penrose RN Rtd.,
13 May 1954,
Burnaston,
Derbyshire.

Commander Horatio Penrose, RN retired, glanced around his black Vauxhall Wyvern saloon as he drove towards his Birmingham home and nodded with satisfaction. All ship-shape and Bristol fashion, he thought, glad he had not agreed to sell the vehicle after all.

He had taken tea with a couple near Buxton who had expressed great interest in purchasing his one year old motor car and after chatting until 10.30 p.m. he told them he felt he wanted to keep the car after all and prepared for the drive home.

They were disappointed, but graciously accepted his decision not to see his handsome vehicle pass to someone else. The Commander said his farewells and stepped into the dark night.

He took the main Derby-Burton road heading in the direction of Birmingham, an uneventful drive initially with little traffic moving at that time of night. Then, as he approached the Hilton Gravel Works near Burnaston, he suddenly spotted a bright light ahead of him.

'It appeared to be coming towards me,' wrote the Commander, who penned a full account of his experience shortly after.

At first he assumed the approaching light was an on-coming car travelling at high speed and he slowed down his vehicle in anticipation of a near miss.

As he braked, the light appeared to come to a sudden halt above him, causing his car to stop so abruptly that he was thrown forward in the driving seat, hitting his head on the windscreen.

'I thought I had been in a crash,' said the Commander who then remembered a sensation of movement. The car felt as if it was rising, being lifted through the air by something magnetic. He could see the metal roof of the vehicle being distorted by the pull of whatever it was.

Craning his neck, he peered through the car window to see

what was above the roof. He couldn't see any lifting gear, despite straining his eyes. But he thought he could see a very bright light positioned directly above the car.

At that point the Commander lost consciousness. He remembers waking in a hospital bed in Derbyshire Royal Infirmary where nursing staff told him he had received stitches to a cut on his forehead.

As he lay back, counting his lucky stars to have survived, he found he could clearly remember the chain of strange events that occurred immediately after the 'crash', so strange he dared not tell anyone of those memories, yet.

After his car had come to an abrupt halt and after it had somehow been lifted into the air, he rembered, it was then lowered onto the side of the road. A man, in a one piece suit, leaned in through the window and lifted the officer from his seat, apparently without effort, pulled him out into the air and up into a large circular object that was hovering directly overhead.

'The entrance was on the underside of this large round vehicle which was giving out a very bright light,' he recalled at the time.

That light enabled him to look down upon the site of the 'crash'. The car was now at the side of the road, but apart from that there was no sign that anything untoward had happened there.

Commander Penrose now found himself in a brightly lit room and was laid on a table. It was some kind of examination table, presumably used for giving medical attention. He looked around and saw the walls of the room were covered in what he took to be control mechanisms. The controls were being operated by a group of men and women, about five of them in all.

They did not appear unusual, apart from being of slightly shorter height than average, more like the Japanese. They also had slightly almond-shaped eyes and their hair was dark and worn short and straight. They all wore blue, one-piece suits.

One of the female operators, attractive and shapely, approached and looked at his injuries. The commander felt this woman, who was probably in her early twenties, looked

Elsie becomes part of UFO team

By Maxine Burrage

A WOMAN from Church Stowe who had a mysterious experience with an Unidentified Flying Object has become a UFO investigator.

Mrs Elsie Oakensen recently told the Daventry Express of her "fascinating" encounter with a UFO nine years ago which will be featured in the book "Abduction", due out in Spring.

And as a member of the recently formed Northamptonshire Unidentified Flying Object Research Centre (NUFORC), Mrs Oakensen has become the Daventry area contact for local sightings.

NUFORC aim to encourage investigation and research into UFO phenomena and to collect information on the subject. Any reports of sightings of UFOs, will be passed from Mrs Oakensen to the investigators who will look into them at depth.

"They are a group of very serious and dedicated people," said Mrs Oakensen. "The team will see anybody who has had a sighting.

"They ask all kinds of questions to work out the angle of the sighting, the height and to work out how big it was", she added. The weather is also taken into account and they also ask if there were any sounds.

"The team contact all airports around to see if it was an aircraft. They go into it scientifically and thoroughly, then report to the British Unidentified Flying Object Research Association," she added.

The research centre is

Call to report sightings

very keen for people to pass on their experiences. Mrs Oakensen said: "They handle everything both sympathetically and in confidence, if that is what the person wishes".

Mrs Oakensen recently made an appearance on BBC 1's 'Kilroy', along with top experts in the country on UFOs.

Although she was invited on the programme to tell the story of her mysterious encounter her opportunity did not arise.

"It was well worth the visit as I met many of the top people in UFOs. Anybody who was anybody in UFOs was there," she said.

"I learnt quite a lot about UFOs. I never thought of my sighting as being anything special, but apparently it was. In UFO circles, my sighting was classed as an abduction because I lost ten minutes in time," she added.

Top & Right: Daventry Weekly Express, December 3, 1987
Top Left: Elsie Oakensen. Above Left: Graham Allen.

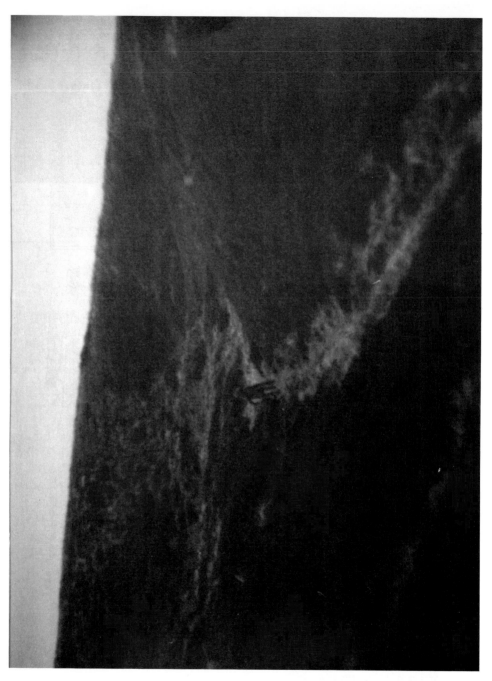

*Above: The 'entity' photograph taken by Philip Spencer on Ilkley Moor,
West Yorkshire December 1, 1987.
Copyright Peter Hough.*

sympathetic as she examined the injury on his forehead and his other minor cuts and bruises.

As she leaned over him he noticed her flawless white skin but before he could comment he realised she was speaking to him about his injuries. It was some form of telepathic communication. He seemed to know what she wanted to know and she seemed to know his answer before he spoke it.

The female gave him an injection and he saw that the syringe she used contained a green fluid of some sort.

'I asked questions about the mechanics of their vehicle,' recalled the Commander later. 'I was told it involved magnetic fields.'

As he tried to make sense of the information communicated to him the female began to ask questions. What was his position, she asked.

The Commander replied cautiously. Could his benefactors be from some foreign power? She seemed terribly interested in his work with the Royal Navy, thought the seasoned serviceman, only too aware that the last war had ended less than a decade ago.

Further questions followed about his naval experiences and his work with radar (then a relatively new technology).

He tried to steer the conversation from himself and asked further questions about the craft and its engineering.

But the female, similarly, avoided direct answers .

For some reason the female then volunteered a curious statement that left the Commander puzzled.

The words she put into his mind were clear: 'We are not born in the same manner as you.'

Around that point Commander Penrose remembered feeling drowsy. 'That injection must have been a sedative,' he thought before drifting off into unconsciousness.

When he came round he was back in his car and feeling groggy. The car had been moved. It was now perched on the gravel works' railings.

It was just before midnight when a passing RAC patrolman spotted the wreckage and found the concussed major sitting in the driver seat. He called the police who interviewed the officer about the incident. But Penrose decided not to mention either the strange craft or its occupants.

Puzzled by the relentless questioning of the officers, he made inquiries and learned that they had been suspicious about the abnormally large amount of blood they found in the wreckage. It seemed far more than the amount one would expect to lose as the result of the relatively minor injuries sustained by the Commander. Some officers suspected he had not been alone.

After his discharge from hospital the officer returned to the scene of the accident in the hope that he might trace witnesses.

His only success was a railway signalman who said he had seen a 'car' with an extremely bright light above it go past his signal box.

Commander Penrose remained silent about his encounter for a staggering twenty two years. Then in 1976 he made contact with a Birmingham UFO research group and told his full story for the first time.

The Commander said he had avoided publicity because he feared the attendant ridicule. By 1976, he said, the climate regarding UFO research had improved sufficiently for him to 'come out'.

Commander Penrose, was an 'old salt' with an exemplary military record. Could the crash, or whatever happened that night, have put his mind off course? Investigators doubt it.

Furthermore his description of the craft, and its occupants, is not too different from the many other reports that have followed since.

Horatio Penrose, officer and gentleman, grew up long before UFOs and flying saucers entered our language. Back in 1954 spaceflight was sci-fi; UFOs and aliens were pure comic-strip fantasy.

Why would a Royal Navy Commander concoct such a story?

Albert Lancashire,
September 1942,
Newbiggin-on-Sea,
Northumberland.

Albert Lancashire shivered in the perishing cold. Winter had come early. The twenty seven year old sentry shoved his hands deeper into the pockets of his Army issue overcoat. Still, guarding this secret radar base against the Luftwaffe was an important job, he mused gazing out over the North Sea.

'It's hard to believe it's only September,' Albert said to himself, stamping his feet to get the circulation going. 'Must be the flamin' wind coming off the sea.'

He had no idea what time it was, but it was very dark. It was important to remember the standing order, he reminded himself, repeating the Captain's instructions out loud: 'Do not fire at enemy aircraft as you will only give away the position of the base.'

Firing at night would be worse, he thought. Gerry pilots would soon spot them and that would be the end of the installation.

Suddenly Albert spotted a light on the horizon, but within seconds a black cloud moved over and obscured it. Then another light moved into his field of view. A yellow light this time, shining from the rim of a strange round object.

Now it was closer, the beam of yellow light, about a foot in diameter, swung round straight into his face.

His jaw dropping, Albert instinctively threw his hands into the air.

'I don't remember putting my rifle down, but I must have because it was loaded and had a bayonet attached,' recalled Albert. 'I didn't use the rifle because we weren't allowed to. I just put my hands up.'

A floating sensation overcame the young serviceman, then blackness.

Albert came to, shocked and dazed, lying only yards from the spot where he had been standing guard just a few minutes earlier.

'I lay there for five or ten minutes,' said Albert. 'I didn't know what had happened.'

Back then Albert didn't call the object he had seen a flying saucer. The term would not come into being for another five years. But he somehow knew that the object he had seen was unnatural, not of this world.

His conviction that something unusual occurred was reinforced by a series of dreams that disturbed his sleep in the following years. He remembers looking down at the sea through a large window and a man in white telling him he had to carry him into the ship.

Then in another dream he is again on the ship and this time meets a woman in a calf length skirt. She has red hair and she gives him some goggles.

It was not until the late sixties that Albert's story came to light. He had been reading about a spate of UFO sightings and wrote to BUFORA about his wartime experience. Sadly the time gap between the event and his reporting of it made investigation difficult.

Albert was in his seventies and living in Denton, Manchester when he last recalled that brief encounter. Having retired from British Rail and with more time on his hands, he has devoured every piece of UFO literature he could get hold of.

He has also developed a great interest in religious matters and all things psychic.

Whether he really was Britain's first real abductee, we will never know, but it is significant that Albert feels that alien abduction is the only phenomenon that fits the bill . . . even after so many years.

June Rice,
August 1956,
Filey,
North Yorkshire.

Jovial granny June Rice dropped her paper in shock as she listened to the radio programme. It was a discussion about UFOs and alien abductions. They were talking about people who had claimed to have been abducted by strange beings who had taken them off in spaceships.

June thought she was the only woman in the world to have been inside a spaceship. The only woman to have met visitors from other worlds.

She scurried off into the kitchen of her neat-as-a-pin home in Wallasey, Merseyside and busied herself by making a cup of tea. Her head was spinning. Could there really be other people who had seen what she had seen? She had always been too afraid to talk openly about what happened to her all those years ago, afraid of the ridicule.

But if other people had experienced what she had seen then maybe she could find out more about those strange visitors. Maybe there was an organisation that could help.

Without revealing her reasons, June made inquiries about UFO organisations and soon got hold of the number for the British UFO Research Association. She picked up her phone and dialled the number.

The voice at the other end seemed friendly so she just blurted it out: 'I was abducted by aliens in 1956 . . .'

When two researchers, including one of the writers, visited June a few days later, they were struck by her friendly, bubbly nature. A doting mum and grandmother, her living room was full of family snaps and she was eager to point out her children and grandchildren of whom she was obviously so proud.

At first she seemed a little embarrassed about what she had experienced all those years ago when she was a young mum with an eighteen month old son, but after some encouragement she agreed to tell her story.

It was during the warm summer of 1956 and June was staying at her mum's house in Filey in North Yorkshire.

'It must have been August,' she remembered. 'A friend and I went out to the pictures one night and when we came out we decided to take the easy way home, which was across the fields.'

'We walked together for some distance until we got near to where she lived. Her house was on one side of the fields and my mum's was on the other. We parted company and I set off for home on my own.'

'It was quiet, unusually quiet that night. You could normally see lots of bats in those fields, but not that night.'

'I was walking along, and it was quite dark by now, and these two men seemed to appear from nowhere. One minute there was nothing and the next these two men were there. They seemed to come towards me, stop and then stand there.'

'They didn't say anything and I didn't. I wasn't frightened. I wasn't scared at all.'

'They were quite tall and had whitish or silver suits on, like an all-in-one suit. It was a long time ago but I remember thinking they were very pale, very. They had lovely eyes, beautiful eyes and white hair.'

'I don't know if they had any beards or anything, but I'll always remember the white hair and the beautiful eyes.'

'Then they just turned and I knew they wanted me to go with them, so I just followed them and then I don't remember anything.'

June can't explain the gap in her memory, but it is a classic case of doorway amnesia, a condition reported by many abductees who rarely remember actually entering the UFO they see.

June found herself in a round room, again this ties in with many later accounts where witnesses often report alien rooms as rounded, seamless and without corners.

Although June never saw a UFO throughout her experience, she is convinced she was inside a craft belonging to the strangers she met.

'The room was completely circular with seats all around and there were people sitting on the seats. They sat me down on one and I remember that by that time I was getting a bit agitated. I had the baby at home, you see, and I said, "No I'm not staying, I want to go home".'

'They never spoke at all and I was saying "No, no, no". Then I realised I wasn't using my mouth to speak. It seemed as if we were communicating through our brains, you know, and I was upset about this.

'One of the people then just came up to me and put his hand on my head and I seemed to go backwards, the seat seemed to come upwards. All I remember from that part of things was a pain in my side.

'I cried out with the pain when this, this whatever it was did something to me. I don't know if something was piercing my skin or what but I was suddenly in my bed back at home.

'I just grabbed hold of my baby and hugged him and I thought 'Where have I been, where have I been?

'I couldn't remember coming home or coming into the house and I had no idea what time it was.'

The next morning June's mother pointed out that she had been out late the previous night.

June didn't say anything. She couldn't. She didn't have a clue of the time when she came in and climbed into bed. But she clearly remembered leaving the cinema at a reasonable time.

June put the incident at the back of her mind and got on with her life, what seemed to be her very normal life.

But when carefully questioned by BUFORA investigators it appeared that June may have had several sightings after that first incident.

Her recollections were often vague and therefore difficult to check, but it appeared she had experienced further missing time episodes.

June had not recorded dates or times in connection with the follow up episodes and although the investigators were convinced of her genuine sincerity there was insufficient data on the episodes for any meaningful investigation.

Going back to that first experience the Ufologists asked June if the events of that night felt physically real.

'Oh yes, yes, it was real,' she replied.

What did she think happened to her?

'I don't know. I think they examined me but I don't know what they did. I know when he put his hand on my head I felt very calm.'

Taking her back to the room inside the craft, the investigators asked if June could describe any of the other people she said she had seen sitting in the seats around the room.

'I remember seeing a nurse sitting there and I remember an airman but there were four or five people in all,' she said. 'They were human beings, yes. They were just sitting there in a daze. They didn't speak to me at all.

'The ones in the nurse's uniform and the RAF uniform stood out.'

How had that event in the summer of 1956 affected her life? 'I believe in UFOs,' said June. 'I believe there's somewhere they're coming from. Where I don't know. I never even thought about UFOs in those days. I don't think there were any then, were there?'

In the days after her encounter June became ill. Lethargy and nausea seemed to make her life a misery so she decided to see a doctor.

'I discovered I was pregnant,' she said. 'The whole pregnancy was a nightmare too. I felt terrible throughout and after giving birth I lost a lot of weight and continued to feel ill for some time.

'I used to think why me? I didn't know anyone else who had been aboard a UFO.'

It was nine months after her meeting with the strangers in the field that June gave birth to her daughter. She often jokes: 'I don't know whether I was pregnant then or whether they impregnated me.

'My daughter says she always knew she didn't belong to this earth.'

For some women that bizarre scenario is not a joke, as you will read later . . .

Gerry Armstrong,
July 1953,
Home Counties.

Twelve year old Gerry Armstrong looked over his shoulder to make sure the coast was clear, then dug into his trouser pocket for the new pack of five Woodbines. Sitting in the shadow of a tree which gave him some welcome shade from the fierce afternoon sun, he fished out his matches, drew out a cigarette and lit-up, his first of the day.

'Who wants to play hide and seek with old Rice anyway,' he said to himself smiling. He thought it was quite smart of him to sneak away as he did, right under his teacher's nose.

Gerry was one of a party of London school kids on a summer camp just outside the capital. His teacher, Mr Rice, had made sure he and his chums were kept fully occupied but the game of hide and seek was just too much for the independent-minded Gerry.

When his teacher had been looking the other way he simply sidled off in the direction of a wooded area.

Now he was far enough away he couldn't hear the shouts of his school pals so he stretched out on the grass, eyes fixed on the clear blue sky and enjoyed his smoke.

The heat of the day had taken it's toll and Gerry was beginning to feel drowsy. He tried to stop himself nodding off, then suddenly he was in darkness.

'Get up Armstrong, where do you think you've been boy?' Gerry opened his eyes with a start. A furious red faced Mr Rice was bellowing in his face.

Why was he so angry? He'd only been away a few minutes.

The he followed his teacher's gaze. He was staring at the half-smoked cigarette which was still stuck between his two fingers in his right hand.

'Get yourself up lad,' screamed the teacher. 'I want to know what you've been up to. We've been searching for you all afternoon and I want some answers.'

Gerry was astonished to learn it was now after 8 p.m. Mr Rice and his school pals had been scouring the countryside for him for hours.

They had even searched the spot where he was now, but there had been no sign of him a little while ago.

Gerry tried to get up but his legs gave way under him. Helped by some of his classmates he managed to hobble back to camp where he was checked over by a doctor.

The back of his neck was red and sore, his pupils were dilated and he was exhausted. Diagnosis: mild sunstroke. The youngster was packed off to bed.

Gerry Armstrong completely forgot about the fuss surrounding his mystery disappearance during that school camp until ten years later when he and his wife sited a UFO near London.

The event triggered his memory of the seven hours that went missing from his own life on that day, but he still couldn't recall where he was or what he had been doing for that period.

Gerry's UFO encounters continued and became more frequent after he emigrated to the Lake Simcoe area of Ontario, Canada. And it was a hypnotherapist from Toronto who enabled him to recover the lost memories from that summer's day in 1953.

The fully qualified psychiatrist decided to put Gerry into regressive hypnosis in a series of sessions throughout 1978. The following account is a compilation of the memories that came back to him.

As he sat under the tree, enjoying his cigarette, Gerry's attention was caught by a bright light in the sky that seemed to descend to a point beyond a nearby clump of trees.

Within minutes the lad thought he could detect some movement through the foliage and, glancing in the direction in which the bright light had appeared to land, he could make out two figures walking in his direction.

For some reason he cannot explain, Gerry was frightened. He wanted to run. The fear grew into terror when he discovered that he could not move. Time and again he tried to move his legs, to put out his arm, but his limbs just would not respond to the messages his brain was sending out to them.

Gerry began to cry. He didn't understand what was going on but he was very frightened.

The figures were now very close. As they closed on him

the youngster was aware of voices in his head. Voices that were telling him not to be afraid, that no harm would come to him. Now the strangers were with him, one positioned on either side of him. They picked him up and began carrying him away. 'It was like floating through the air' thought the child, trying to laugh out loud to show that he wasn't scared.

As he floated through the trees, he could see a bright light in a clearing ahead of him, so bright it hurt his eyes. The object took on a vaguely rounded shape as he neared it, although the intensity of the light made it difficult to work out what it was.

To rest his eyes from the assault of light, Gerry turned to his captors. They were small (one was smaller than the boy who was probably four and a half feet) and they had white-grey skins, small mouths and prominent eyes.

At last they reached the object. Gerry, who had now re-gained the use of his limbs, was instructed to climb the ladder which seemed to lead up to an entrance. As he began to do so he felt a momentary severe pressure on the back of his neck, caused, he assumed, by something the strangers did.

Once inside the strange object, he found himself alone and in a brightly lit room with no apparent source for the light. As he explored the chamber he felt a strange sensation and accompanying noise and seemed to know that the object, or craft, was moving.

After a while the beings returned and led Gerry along a semi-corridor to another room where he met a being dressed in red. The youngster thought this person seemed older than the other two, and he was amused by the way the being addressed him as 'my son'.

Gerry was instructed to look at a screen on the wall. He saw what he first described as a 'little ball'. But on closer examination he could see it was a planet.

'This is your home,' said a voice in his head. The sudden realisation that he was looking back at earth was too much for young Gerry. Once again he was gripped by fear at the thought of being so far away from home.

The being in red, seemingly realising the boy's distress,

reached over and touched Gerry's forehead. Immediately the fear was replaced by calmness.

At that point he realised the noise that had started soon after entering the object had stopped . Had the craft landed somewhere? The two strangers who had brought him on board and the being in red indicated as they began to walk down a ramp that Gerry should accompany them. An automatic door opened at the end of the ramp at which point the boy found himself looking out at the inside of a giant dome.

'It's full of children,' said Gerry as he saw many youngsters walking this way and that before him. The voice in his head told him to be calm and to follow the being in red.

At which point the being put something into Gerry's hand. 'It's like a ball,' said the youngster. But it was much more than a ball. On instruction from his captors Gerry looked at the spherical gadget and saw his life flash before him.

'Understand, be taught,' said the voices in his head. The boy now seemed to be alone, so set off to explore his new surroundings. He studied the building itself and noticed the dome was mauve and transparent. Through it he could see strange craft travelling through the dark sky, craft that he thought might not be unlike the object he had travelled here in.

A woman approached him, breaking the reverie, and took hold of the silver cross that hung round his neck on a chain. he had taken it from his mother's jewellery box before leaving home for summer camp.

The woman passed the cross to the being in red and both studied it. Their words formed in Gerry's brain: 'It's not right to worship'.

They indicated he should study his screen, the ball-like device, once more. The being in red touched the boy's head and he slept.

Gerry awoke to find himself being carried through the woodland area where he had first seen the strangers.

He was frightened again, but not of the strangers, now of the reaction he would get from Mr Rice.

The beings set him down in the spot where they had found him. Gerry was surprised to see his cigarette was still there, burning although the sky was now getting dark. The strangers said farewell leaving Gerry alone once again.

Still tired, Gerry drifted off to sleep again. Until . . .

'Get up Armstrong,' roared Mr Rice . . .

IS IT ALL IN THE MIND?

Explanations for abduction phenomena are legion but the vast majority of the so-called rational theories fall under the umbrella of 'psychological explanations'.

And the numbers of papers written on the subject by psychologists from around the world with a whole range of theories must run into hundreds.

One research team actually said recently that abductees fell into a class of the population they labelled FPP, fantasy-prone personalities. This group of people (the researchers estimated they could account for up to four per cent of the population) were categorised as excellent hypnotic subjects who were prone to fantasising in both childhood and adulthood and who regarded themselves as psychic or telepathic, experienced out-of-body experiences, had vivid dreams and often felt the ability to heal.

Well, like most psychological explanations for abduction phenomenon, you can read into it what you will.

Abductions are fair game for psychologists. They don't have to commit themselves one way or the other. The phenomenon is a fascinating one – normal, rational, healthy individuals reporting the most abnormal, irrational events.

If a university will fund the research, the psychologist will spend many happy hours pondering whether the witness encountered a UFO complete with aliens or merely perceived an encounter with a UFO and aliens. Then he will write his paper listing the various psychological options available and move on to the next project. He does not have to put his professional neck on the line. He's not going to say human beings ARE being abducted by aliens in UFOs but then he doesn't have to commit himself and say people are NOT being space-napped by little green men.

Sadly that does not help poor Mr or Mrs X who may have had their worlds turned inside out by what to them is a real abduction. They may have seen a UFO, had an encounter with an alien, been taken into a strange craft.

If they are suffering from some type of psychological disorder then it appears there are a lot of people like them.

We have already said that the number of alleged abductees of which we know is substantial. The number may in reality be far greater. And new abduction reports are coming into UFO research organisations almost every day.

However the psychological link is tempting. Many abductees claim they have further encounters with UFOs or aliens after their initial abduction. A large proportion also claim to have had psychic experiences in the past and others, like Elsie Oakensen, say that they have developed powers, like healing, after their experience.

The fact that many abductees claim multiple abductions over a succession of years implies they are prone to the experience. And if they are prone to such events surely we should be studying them and not their experiences.

'Nonsense,' says Budd Hopkins, New York artist and renowned UFO investigator whose theory of alien genetic experimentation is built around the reported selection of human individuals for genetic testing. He believes the fact that a number of witnesses report several abductions supports his theory.

The many similarities between abduction victims led British investigator Ken Phillips to launch the ill-fated *Anamnesis Project*.

The London maths teacher and researcher with the British UFO Research Association could not help but notice those similarities during his years interviewing possible abductees.

He had been struck by the number of individuals who had experienced psychic events or displayed Extra-Sensory Projection abilities.

He had been impressed by the work of Dr Alex Keul, the psychologist and Austrian representative of the international research group the Mutual UFO Network. When Keul realised that vital data on UFO witnesses was virtually non-existent, he devised a protocol called Anamnesis – life memory.

The anamnesis is a sixty page plus questionnaire which asks for information about the witness's health, beliefs, dreams and previous anomalous experiences in order to gather a fuller picture of the individual. Only this way could one discover whether the same type of person was reporting the same type of incident.

As Ken Phillips puts it: 'Instead of looking out of the window with the witness in the direction of whatever it was that had long since appeared and departed, we were now looking back through the window at the witness in order to profile who is doing the perceiving and reporting.'

Ken began the daunting task of collecting the mass of information necessary for the Anamnesis Project.

One of the most interesting facts thrown up by early analysis of the data was that more people than allowed by mere chance were dissatisfied with their treatment by society. This social dissatisfaction trend was also echoed in the number of encounter witnesses who tended to be loners.

However it was soon realised that the statistics being collected were relatively useless unless they could be compared to the results from a control group. The anamnesis reports were on people who had all had some sort of UFO encounter, otherwise they would not have come to the attention of BUFORA.

At present, the project is on ice while Ken and his colleagues reconsider their approach.

One of the most exciting new approaches to the alien abduction enigma comes from Albert Budden, a former member of the scientific civil service and science teacher.

He joined a UFO research group as an investigator fourteen years ago after 'encounters' experienced by his wife led him to become interested.

'My wife had not been an abductee but had suffered a number of hallucinations, figures appearing before her and so on,' said Albert. 'I wanted to know more and began to investigate other cases.'

Like others before him, he was struck by the number of alleged abductees who had also had psychic experiences, out-of-body experiences and other anomalous effects.

But unlike others, he came up with a theory based on allergies and embarked on years of gruelling research, poring over scores of scientific papers and interviewing the experts until he was confident that his idea was valid.

In a recently published paper *Allergies and Aliens*, he maintains that abduction victims are a group of hypersensitives who react to certain conditions by hallucinating.

But the group of people he has identified are not simply allergic to certain foods or substances – but to a whole range of environmental conditions, including electro-magnetic radiation.

'I believe some people are electro-magnetic hypersensitives,' he said recently speaking from his Brentford home. 'There is a great deal of electronic pollution in the world, from radio frequencies to emissions from aerials, mobile phones, emergency services communications networks and so on.

'People sensitive to these fields of electro-magnetic energy can, in the most extreme cases, experience hallucinations. These may be reported as UFO abductions or ghosts or other psychic events.

'I discovered during my days as an investigator that the people who reported UFO abductions were nearly always sensitives in one way or another. A great many suffered from various allergies and the chances are that they have a sensitivity to electromagnetic forces.'

He believes that it is more than coincidental that UFO abduction reports did not start until the early 1960s, the beginning of the communications revolution. His theory would also go some way to explaining why the great majority of UFO and alien abduction reports come from sophisticated, technologically advanced western nations where electronic pollution would be at its greatest.

'The level of electro-magnetic activity depends on many things including geography,' said Albert, who believes other forms of environmental pollution may also play its part.

Albert also says exposure to a natural phenomena known as earthlights, balls of electro-magnetic energy that can rise from the earth's crust via natural faults, can also have a major effect on people.

'The way people change after abduction experience is amazing,' said Albert. 'People can change their diet, become vegetarians, stop smoking.

'Take the Aveley case. The green fog they went through

was an electrical mist caused by the electrification of water beneath a line of pylons nearby.

'After that incident the husband and wife went through some great changes in lifestyle and the young son who went through them found a dramatic improvement in his reading ability afterwards.

'It is my contention that the electro-magnetic energy has done something to the brain. This is where the neurologists come in because we don't know what happens inside the body to cause these changes.'

Albert believes up to twenty per cent of the population could be hypersensitive to their environment.

His book, out next year, *UFOs – The Electromagnetic Indictment* is bound to cause a flurry in academic circles as well as in the world of Ufology.

Even if Albert's theories prove correct and an allergic reaction to the environment is responsible for alien abduction reports, why do so many people see such similar things? Why don't we hallucinate about scoring the winning goal in the Cup Final, or being shipwrecked on a desert island or a million and one other things?

Is the influence of UFOs and flying saucer folklore so great in our society that our minds immediately latch onto it to explain bizarre hallucinations?

Decide for yourself whether the following cases fall in with Albert Budden's idea.

The first case is probably one of the best known in British Ufology and has had a wide airing in the media.

PC Alan Godfrey,
28 November 1980,
Todmorden,
West Yorkshire.

It was 5.15 a.m. and PC Alan Godfrey was near to finishing his shift. In the past few hours he had been called to an estate in Burnley Road following reports that a herd of thirty cows had been roaming around. He hadn't found them so now he was returning for a final check before heading back to the station.

As he was about to turn off the A646, the main Burnley to Todmorden road, he caught a glimpse of a strange glow about two hundred yards away. He drove on to investigate.

Astonished by the intensely bright, almost diamond-shaped object before him he brought his Ford Escort panda car to a halt. The thing was now about one hundred feet away.

The rain that had teemed down throughout the night had now stopped and PC Godfrey had a clear uninterrupted view of the bizarre sight. It was dome-shaped with a top which was flatter than the base. Fluorescent light issued from the top and he could see a row of dark but square windows beneath the light.

The top portion of the craft remained still, the bottom portion rotated as the puzzled policeman watched the head-lights from his patrol car reflecting on its shiny white surface. PC Godfrey resisted the temptation to climb out of his patrol car for a closer look on foot. He felt a sense of security in the familiar surroundings of his vehicle and although there was only a windscreen between him and the unknown he was loathe to get any closer. Instead he used his trained police-man's eye to estimate the dimensions of the object. About twenty feet in diameter, he judged, based on the way it spanned the road width. Hovering about five feet above the road surface it could not have been much more than twelve or fourteen feet high. The officer noticed, to his further amaze-ment, the leaves on some adjacent trees shaking wildly despite the fact that the dark morning air was completely still, with no hint of a breeze.

'There was no doubt that what I was looking at was real,' he said at the time. 'It was no illusion. If I had got out of my car and thrown a brick at it, it would have gone bang.'

The constable decided to report into the station. First he tried the car radio, but it was dead. The he reached for his personal walky-talky. Both VHF and UHF were silent, devoid even of the static that normally plagued the airwaves.

Determined to somehow record the sight before him the policeman grabbed his clipboard and sketched the object as best he could on an official police accident form.

Suddenly the officer looked up and the object was gone. He was several hundred yards further down the road than where he had been, and he was driving.

He had no idea how he got there, no recollection of putting the car in gear and setting off. One minute he was sitting in his parked patrol car sketching the strange object before him. The next he was driving through a dark and empty night. But he did seem to remember hearing a voice in his head say: 'You should not be seeing this . . . It is not for your eyes . . . You will forget it.'

PC Godfrey stopped his vehicle and looked behind him almost to confirm that the UFO had indeed gone, then drove back into Todmorden town centre.

Seeing a colleague he stopped his car and gave him a brief run down of what he had seen. Together they drove back to the spot where he had seen the object.

The place was deserted, the UFO had left no permanent marks. However, PC Godfrey and his colleague saw blotchy patches on the road surface over which it had hovered, in contrast to the uniform wetness of the road surface.

This was hardly evidence of an unusual event. Evaporation would soon eliminate the whirlpool-shaped marks directly beneath the spot where the strange, domed contraption had hovered.

Looking down at his feet, the officer noticed a split in his boot, as if it had been dragged along the ground. That hadn't been there at the beginning of his shift, of that he was sure.

PC Godfrey decided to keep the report of his astonishing encounter to himself – until the following day when he discovered that three officers on the moors had reported a brilliant light heading towards Todmorden on the night of his own sighting.

Emboldened by the news he decided to file his report and it wasn't long before a team from the Manchester UFO Research Association became involved.

PC Godfrey's story attracted publicity in the local and national press and was followed by a book which detailed the results of hypnotic regression on the thirty three year old police officer.

During that session he recalled a meeting with a tall humanoid being by the name of Yoseph and a medical examination conducted by a group of smaller beings, less than four feet in height.

In a telepathic conversation his abductors revealed that they knew him, indicating that there may be more to other previous periods of missing time which he could recall.

This was not PC Godfrey's first encounter with the odd.

In the summer of that year he had been involved in another mystery when he discovered a body lying on top of a twenty foot high pile of coal in a railway goods yard in Todmordon.

The body was identified as that of fifty six year old Polish miner Zygmund Adamski, who had disappeared from home five days earlier.

A post mortem revealed that he had died of a heart attack, but could not find any reason for the burns marks on his head and back which had apparently been caused by some corrosive liquid.

The mystery led to wild claims about a mystery death with some so-called enthusiastic UFO watchers claiming Mr Adamski's body could only have been lowered onto the tip from above . . . presumably from a flying saucer.

Serious Ufologists have never claimed any significance in the Adamski death and have been embarrassed by the unfounded claims from some quarters.

PC Godfrey survived that investigation. But the publicity surrounding his own encounter was too much for his employers who questioned his fitness for duty.

In the end Alan Godfrey was forced to retire from the force, with honour.

That would have been the end of the Godfrey story except

for the fact that a witness came forward who claimed to have seen the police officer being escorted into an alien craft eleven months *before* the alleged abduction . . .

From: C R Neville
        Secretariat (Air Staff)2a

        MINISTRY OF DEFENCE Room 8245
        Main Building Whitehall London SW1A 2HB

        Telephone 01-218 2140 (Direct Dialling)
                  01-218 9000 (Switchboard)

Mr P Mantle   Your reference

                                         Our reference
                                         D/Sec(AS)12/3
                                         Date
                                         19 November 1989

Dear Mr Mantle

Thank you for your letter of 24 October, in which you requested a copy of a report of an unusual sighting witnessed by P C Alan Godfrey on 28 November 1980, in Todmorden, West Yorkshire.

Although I must confess that P C Godfrey's name rings a bell (perhaps his sighting was mentioned in a newspaper article?), I regret that a search through our files has not revealed a copy of this particular report.

I am sorry that I cannot be of help on this occasion.

Yours faithfully

Above: Letter to Philip Mantle from Ministry of Defence.

William Barrett,
14 January 1980,
Heald Moor,
Lancashire.

Lorry driver William Barrett had a big job on that day. He had to pick up a large load of yarn from Courtauld's Mill at Hollingworth near Oldham, so he set off from his Burnley home well before 6 a.m. to give himself plenty of time to negotiate the treacherous ice bound roads of the Yorkshire/ Lancashire border.

William had to drop off a package at Todmorden en route so he took the A646 Burnley to Todmorden route which follows the River Calder as it winds its way through the windswept foothills of the Pennines.

It was a bitterly cold morning with no moon or stars to relieve the darkness, only a mass of dark clouds overhead threatening snow.

The fifty five year old former Royal Marine had only been on the road for twenty minutes when he crossed the railway bridge at Heald Moor which is approximately mid-way between Burnley and Pendle. It was at this point that he first heard the humming.

The deep humming, similar to the noise made by an electricity generator was quite clear. William could easily distinguish it from the not inconsiderable noise made by his engine despite the fact that the windows in the cab were fully closed.

But William didn't have time to worry about the strange sound. Seconds after it began the beams of his vehicle's headlights picked out an odd shape in the lay-by ahead.

'What's going on here?' William asked himself as he looked at what first reminded him of a giant toast rack. It was dark, metallic and had three red 'rays' projecting from the top down to the ground. The whole thing was resting on the ground, not moving.

'I was quite relaxed about it,' recalled William later. 'There were people moving about and I took them to be workmen making an early start. I thought they might be getting a machine ready to lay tar on the road.'

As the distance between the object and his truck closed,

William's view improved. The machine, if that is what it was, looked more tortoise-shell in shape and the three beams, now less red, were projected from holes about two thirds of the way up the side of the object.

On its top was a curved 'pipe', which led William to wonder if he was looking at a secret weapon.

He looked for the people he had seen earlier. The two figures, who he could only see as silhouettes against the background light from the object, were moving from side to side, and appeared to be looking at or inspecting the beams.

Reducing his speed to a crawl William peered through the darkness at the figures and saw one was wearing a peaked cap and a dark two-piece uniform. His arms were at his side.

The second figure appeared to be wearing a one-piece suit, grey or silver in colour, and he was stooping down, bending at his knees to look at the object 'as if it had broken down', as William recalled later.

At this point, the closest he got to the scene, William could see the beams were bright. They flickered or rotated causing the silhouettes of the two figures to break-up as they moved in front of them. It reminded the driver of the scintillating effect he had noticed at laser shows. The beams cast a dim reflection on the surface of the object and also caused the bracken on the hillside immediately adjacent to glow an angry red.

As the lorry drew away from the lay-by William continued to glance behind him to see if he could see any further clue to what was going on.

Suddenly he was plunged into darkness. His vehicle's headlights had gone out on the unlit road and he was forced to jam on his brakes to avoid running off the road. As the ten-ton truck ground to a halt William himself blacked out.

A sudden jolting sensation brought the witness back to consciousness. Still in his cab with the engine running he could see his lights were working again.

Scanning his surroundings he immediately knew he had moved. Looking over his shoulder William could see no sign of the lay-by or the object. Later he realised he had been a quarter mile further along the A646 when he came to.

'I just didn't know what had happened,' said William later.

'I didn't know where I was or whether I had been asleep. All I could think of was escape.'

Feeling shaky and light-headed, he put the engine into gear and continued his journey into Todmorden where he now noticed that it was growing light.

He passed the police station but decided against making a report. He dropped off his parcel and continued onto Oldham without stopping.

When he arrived at his destination William was confused to see another delivery vehicle which should have arrived later already there. He asked one of the workmen for the time and was told it was 9.10 a.m.

He was stunned. A journey that should have taken him an hour and a quarter had taken three hours twenty-five minutes. Where had he been during the missing two hours?

William Barret drove home, nagged by a pain in his left leg. He found a bruise mark just behind and above the left knee but had no idea how he had got it. Extremely tired he went to bed and tried to forget about the day's strange events.

However the geography of the encounter came back to haunt him nearly two years later when he read a report of the PC Alan Godfrey incident in a national newspaper.

William was intrigued by a photograph in the newspaper which showed the officer with Mons Mill, a Todmorden landmark in the background. He had passed that very mill after 'waking up' following his own encounter.

Now feeling that he wanted to tell his own story, William wrote to various organisations including a national newspaper, but with no response. Then in 1984 his case landed on the desk of a British UFO Research Association investigator.

Researchers were astonished by William's clear belief that he had witnessed the abduction of PC Alan Godfrey. That would have been impossible as his episode took place nearly a year before the police officer's encounter.

William's interest in the subject had been sparked by press reports of the Godfrey case and he had noticed the vague similarities in Geography. Both cases had occurred on the A646, but several miles, and eleven months apart.

Nevertheless his sighting was thoroughly investigated. And

although no other sightings were reported in the area on that day a similar object was seen at Bradley, just across the border into North Yorkshire the following evening.

Two women reported observing a 'rotating object with two slits down the side which gave off a red glow'.

It would be difficult to come to any firm conclusions about the Barrett case. Reading about the Alan Godfrey abduction obviously coloured his testimony to the extent that he believed the uniformed figure he described was the police officer, a classic case of force-fitting erroneous detail.

The Godfrey case apart, William Barrett saw a strange object, experienced an apparently associated malfunction of his vehicle and reports two hours of missing time.

Rae Fountain,
11 July 1957,
Leighton Buzzard,
Bedfordshire.

Nine year old Rae Fountain was playing hookey that glorious summer's afternoon. As long as he got back for the football match at 5 p.m. he would be okay; they wouldn't miss him.

But he had broken the cardinal rule of his boarding school: never leave the premises without prior permission. If his absence was discovered there would be hell to pay.

Rae found himself down a small, muddy track, bordered by hawthorn and other bushes. Idly scuffing the ground with his boots and regularly glancing at the gleaming new watch on his wrist, a gift on his ninth birthday of two days earlier, he spotted footprints in the drying mud.

The schoolboy typically tried to follow the trail by putting his own feet into the marks in the ground. After following the strange closely-spaced marks for a few yards, he looked at his watch again. It was 3.30 p.m. When he looked up he saw two men ahead of him – possibly the men responsible for the footprints.

The child thought they looked odd, perhaps it was the grey all-in-one boiler suits they wore, or the way they walked in unusually short steps.

Excited by the mystery, Rae darted to the side of the track and tried to hide himself in the bushes. Peering at his quarry, he saw one was about five feet seven inches tall and the other, who he assumed to be a woman, was about a foot shorter.

The pair were completely oblivious to the boy as they carefully picked pieces of twig and berries from the bushes and placed them in a container before them.

Rae couldn't understand why they picked up lumps of mud, pebbles and weeds too.

Stalking them, as children do, Rae darted from bush to bush, but he failed to get a look at their faces. All he could see was their closely cropped brown hair. He was confused by the small, narrow tubes which ran down one side of their heads and into their collars. A green liquid seem to run up and down the tubes as they walked awkwardly forward.

Rae had almost caught up with the two strangers when a blue-tinged object suddenly appeared before them.

'It just swished into view across the track,' recalled Rae much later. 'It was metallic and roughly bell-shaped, about thirty to thirty five feet across, and it just hovered a few feet above the ground.

A door in the rounded top slid open and a ladder was lowered to the ground.

Rae thought he spotted another figure through the open doorway. The two strangers climbed the ladder, entered the object and the door slid shut. The object then shot up vertically for several hundred feet before sweeping across the sky.

The boy's next memory is of a furious headmaster rousing him as he lay in a heap by the side of the road.

'Where have you been boy? Do you realise its 10.30 p.m. and we've had the whole school out searching for you?' Rae looked at his new watch. It still said 3.30 p.m.

After his dressing-down by the headmaster, Rae's school chums pleaded with him for details of what he had been up to. The quiet, introverted lad kept his silence. Yet the boys were convinced he'd been somewhere exciting. They said he was 'sunburned'.

Rae kept his experiences to himself until 1978 when he spoke to an investigator from Contact UK by which time he could relate two further encounters.

One was a sighting of three craft in Scotland and the other was a sighting of UFOs and occupants in Kent. On neither subsequent occasion did he experience missing time although his wrist watch again mysteriously stopped during the Kent encounter.

Was Rae's missing time an abduction?

'He seemed very sincere and pleased to get the encounter off his chest when he spoke,' said the investigator.

And the follow-up sightings tie in with many reports from abductees.

Rosalind Reynolds,
September 1983,
Sudbury,
Suffolk.

Citizens' Band radio fan Ros Reynolds and her then boyfriend
Philip were on a late summer's drive through East Anglia
when an encounter with a UFO changed her life.

The couple had set off from Clacton, Essex to Corby in
Northamptonshire where they were due to meet relatives, but
they had given themselves two and a half hours to reach
their destination so they could enjoy the journey.

They stopped off for a burger shortly after leaving Clacton,
then continued on towards Sudbury through the warm bright
evening with the windows of the car wound down and their
radio tuned into their favourite station.

As they approached the outskirts of Sudbury they found
themselves driving beneath some high tension cables strung
between electricity pylons which march up the adjacent
hillside.

Suddenly they were confronted by a strange configuration
of lights as they emerged from underneath the power lines.

A horse-shoe shaped set of lights was approaching them
at high speed. The multi-coloured, mostly orange and red
object seemed to swoop low over their car.

It was at that moment when Rosalind noticed the silence
and strange stillness around her. As the UFO moved across
the sky a lurid flash of blue electric light illuminated everything around her.

'It made everything look like a photo negative,' recalled
Ros, explaining also how she would never forget the way the
huge electrical tendrils arc-ed their way up the metal skel-
etons of the pylons in that heartstopping moment.

A strange, foul smell, almost like rotten eggs seemed to be
coming from the object. The odour became stronger the
closer it was.

Bemused by the strange light show, the couple pressed on
through Sudbury and at Long Melford joined the A1092 to
Haverhill.

As Philip concentrated on driving his Ford Cortina,

Rosalind took in the surrounding countryside. Then her eye was caught by something in the distance.

'Look another one,' she screamed, pointing to an oval-shaped object that was heading towards the car. 'It's coming towards us.'

'It's probably just a plane, or a helicopter,' grunted Philip, keeping his eyes on the road ahead.

'Why should a plane draw level with us?' she asked as she looked out at the opalescent ball that was now obviously pacing the car. Philip would have none of it; he simply continued to drive through the enfolding darkness of the late evening.

Rosalind tried to ignore the thing that followed them, but it was no good, she knew it was there. Philip refused to acknowledge its existence.

Later Ros said: 'I don't know how long we drove on like that, it could have been twenty minutes, or two hours.'

Suddenly they were plunged into darkness. The car's engine and electrics cut out simultaneously, and the disabled vehicle rolled to a stop.

Philip 'was glued to the steering wheel, looking straight ahead as if he had blinkers on' remembers Ros. She assumed that, like she, he was shocked and scared by the presence of the UFO.

The thing was now so close they could not avoid looking at it.

Big, bright and round and sitting just sixty feet away from their now crippled car. 'It was like a big ball of light with lots of little lights around it,' Ros told an investigator.

The couple reluctantly climbed out of their car and lifted the bonnet to see if they could find the trouble. The way the car had cut out it had seemed as if the battery had been suddenly drained.

As they stood looking into the engine compartment the Cortina's headlamps came on. The couple looked at each other and Phil jumped back in the driver's seat and tried the ignition. It started first time. Ros climbed in and they pulled away with the UFO still flashing nearby.

As they increased the distance between themselves and the strange object the pair seemed to relax. Then a few miles away from their encounter Ros saw what she believes was the same object shooting straight up into the sky with a pencil-thin blue light streaming out behind it.

Glad to be on their way they seemed to make good progress but when they got to Corby their host was not answering the knock at his door.

Suddenly a window above opened, and a head popped out and said: 'What time do you call this? It's half past one in the morning.'

Their two and a half hours journey had taken FIVE AND A HALF HOURS. .

Ros and Phil were stunned by the events of that night, and by their missing hours. But the after-effects of that encounter would be equally astonishing. Within months the couple broke up after six years together. 'He was a different person, not the Philip I knew,' said Ros.

Rosalind had changed too. She dramatically lost weight, despite developing a craving for sweets, especially chocolate, and went down to just six stones.

She gave up drinking and smoking and suddenly became creative, speedily writing papers on such topics as: 'How the universe was formed' and 'What religion really is'.

But she was desperate to discover why she had three hours missing from her life. What had happened on that summer's evening which had changed her life so much ?

Ros saw the chance to recover that lost time when she spotted an article in a local newspaper about an East Anglian UFO research group. She made contact and they arranged a hypnosis session at her home.

But the session went disastrously wrong. 'A bright beam of light came into the room, the video recording was wiped out and all the clocks stopped,' said Ros.

After the abandoned hypnosis session Ros was advised to see a psychic and introduced to the man she would shortly marry, Mark Reynolds-Parnham, who claims to have been psychic since birth.

Mark arranged a second hypnosis session in which Ros was taken back to her 1983 encounter. She recalled being approached by four or five small beings after their car had broken down.

The aliens, for that is what she assumed they were, forced her into their craft.

They took her to an examination room where she was undressed and laid on a clear perspex-like table for observation . . .

Ros became agitated, embarrassed and frightened during the hypnosis session. She had described how the aliens had undressed her and had laid her on the table but then she had become very quiet.

Suddenly Ros sat bolt upright in her chair and screamed: 'No I don't want any babies.'

So concerned were the hypnosis team by Ros's distress in the trance, they decided to bring her back.

Ros is convinced she underwent some gynaecological procedure but she still prefers not to speak about her hypnosis session.

Since that night she has suffered irregular menstruation which she feels has cost her the chance to have children. Medical tests failed to find the cause for the problem

She also reports an unexplained scar in the vaginal area, which she assumed is linked with her alleged abduction. Additionally she developed a 'buzzing in her head' which troubles her to this day.

Rosalind says the after-effects of that encounter were truly devastating for her. The initial weight loss left her friends and family worried that she might be anorexic and she was worried about her missing periods.

'I could not talk to anybody about these things because I thought they would think I was a freak,' said Ros. 'I just bottled it up. I became a recluse for a while worrying about what had happened.'

Her husband Mark has helped her come to terms with her experience, but she now believes she may well have had UFO encounters in the past, short slices of missing time that she simply ignored.

Ernest Jones (pseudonym),
December 1972,
Marlow,
Buckinghamshire.

Publican and ex-RAF man Ernest Jones was heading home
on the A4155 Henley-on-Thames to Marlow road in Buckinghamshire sometime after midnight when he drove into a
mystery that remains with him to this day.

It had been a totally uneventful journey through very light
traffic on a bitterly cold night. As he motored along a half
mile straight section of the road near Mill End he noticed a
bright light ahead of him.

As he approached he could see the light was emanating
from some farm buildings on his near side. Moving closer he
saw the light was in fact some distance from the farm and
coming from an object just ten yards from the roadside.

Hexagonal, or octagonal, the object was approximately the
same size as a public telephone box with a conical top and
strips of powerful fluorescent lighting running down it in a
vertical pattern.

Mr Jones remembers pulling up alongside the object for a
better view; he felt that the UFO was in the process of
landing. A high pitched whistling sound seemed to be coming
from it.

Ernest Jones' next memory was driving through Marlow,
about four miles further down the road and checking his
watch . . . it was one and a half hours later.

Ten years earlier, while serving in the forces, Ernest Jones
had another encounter while parked on moorland overlooking
Holton Airfield in Berkshire.

Sitting in his car with his girlfriend, they watched in aston-
ishment as a large white, revolving object dropped to the
ground, disappearing behind some woodland.

The sudden appearance of the UFO sent his girlfriend into
hysterics so Mr Jones agreed to move on.

He switched on the ignition, but the car's electrical system
seemed dead. Finally he managed to shove the vehicle down
the four hundred yard incline towards the road, at the bottom
of which the lights and the engine burst into life.

Typical of a great many less than dramatic cases, Ernest Jones makes no great claims or assumptions about what happened to him.

But Ufologists feel there are just too many such cases for them to be ignored.

Rohan Hinton,
Summer 1988,
Delaware,
USA.

Twenty three year old Rohan Hinton was just seventeen
when she had her first abduction experience. She had been
having a holiday with her mother and her uncle and aunt at
Chesapeake Bay on the east coast of the United States.

Rohan was familiar with UFO phenomena after both her
uncle and mother had separate experiences. But she was not
prepared for what happened to her in the motel room that
summer.

'We were staying at the beach for a few days,' recalled
Rohan. 'My mum and my aunt and I checked into the hotel
and we got a room with two double beds. My aunt and I were
in one bed and my mother in the other.

'I couldn't sleep because I was feeling stressed. It was
something that bothered me the previous summer when I
was on holiday in the States; I had a UFO sighting and it
stressed me out, it upset me.

'That night I was just lying there gazing at the ceiling of the
motel room and then I heard the voice. It said, "Don't worry,
you are all right, we are not going to bother you because you
cannot deal with it."

'It was a voice in my head, more masculine than feminine
saying: "We are going to leave you alone, you are not strong
enough."

'I felt instantly calm and fell asleep. When I woke up, three
hours later, it was dark but I could see because of the
moonlight coming through the window. I realised I was
floating . . .'

Rohan was high above the bed and could look down on the
sleeping forms of her mother and aunt. She felt as if someone,
some power was holding her aloft. 'The next thing I was in a
bright, bright room and I said "Who put the lights on?"

'They were standing there, standing around me and I was
lying on what felt like a sheet of metal. They were looking at
me in an indulgent way, not hostile. Indulgent, as if looking at
a child.'

Rohan described her visitors as light grey in colour with huge dark eyes.

'It was like looking at a black and white photograph because of their big black eyes and their skin colouring. They were definitely human-like, hairless and with tapering heads.'

Suddenly Rohan was back in the motel room, still floating and then crashed down onto her bed.

'I hit the bed and sort of jerked up shouting "They lied, they lied – they promised that they were going to leave me alone, but they didn't. They tricked me."'

Rohan was convinced her experience was real, not a dream. The strange episodes have continued since. Now a personal assistant to a managing director of a London company. Rohan lives in a flat in Dulwich, East London, which has been the scene for further odd events.

Back in 1992, Rohan was sharing her home with a boyfriend, Andy, who was in the habit of leaving for work at five in the morning.

'It was about December or January and I woke up at about six in the morning. Someone was moving about in the hallway and I thought it must be Andy come back to collect something he had forgotten.

'The light in the hall was on and I raised my head to look and then this thing just shuffled into the bedroom. It was thin with a thin face and very large eyes and it just shuffled over to the futon I was lying on and touched me with this incredibly long finger.

'I felt as if I was falling backwards, just like passing out . . .'

Rohan awoke to find her mystery visitor had vanished. 'I remember thinking at the moment that it touched me, "Oh my God this is really happening". There was no doubt that it was real.'

Rohan has had a variety of anomalous experiences since early childhood when she would tell her parents she had seen a mysterious 'grey lady'.

Further disturbed nights at her flat, followed by days of complete exhaustion, caused her to wonder whether she had been taken somewhere during the night.

'I somehow know when I have had an experience the previous night because of the way I feel the next day.'

Rohan has now come to terms with her UFO/abduction experiences and she has turned what some contactees regard as a curse into a party trick.

She explained: 'I was with my boyfriend and another girl the other week and we were standing on the roof of the house having a drink and watching the stars and I said, "I can bring a UFO here".

'They said go on then, so I sort of sent a thought out, into the sky and a few minutes later . . . there it was.

'It was winking and flashing and it moved slowly across the sky.'

Is Rohan Hinton a young woman whose multiple UFO/abduction experiences mean she is of some special interest to extra-terrestrials? Or is she an over-enthusiastic sky-watcher with a well developed imagination?

Theorists like Albert Budden might speculate her wealth of psychic and UFO experiences could make her an electromagnetic hypersensitive.

Psychologists might say her UFO party trick was an indication that she is seeking attention.

Another case for debate.

Mik Burley,
June 1978,
Middlesbrough,
Cleveland.

Mik Burley was in goal for his school on that hot and humid summer's day and the lads were playing hard and fast, determined to score in this important junior fixture.

Mik hadn't been playing long when one of the opposing strikers raced down the field and kicked the heavy leather ball high into the air.

He didn't see it coming. Mik took the full force of the descending ball when it crashed into the side of his face knocking him sideways. 'It rattled my brain and made me feel dizzy.' He was escorted to the side of the pitch where he was laid down to recover. 'I put my head on my arm and looked down, then I just seemed to black out. First there was a bright flash and I was out,' he recalled later.

Mik assumed he was in hospital. He was lying on his back, a figure in a monk's cowl was standing to his right and through blurred vision he saw two or three other figures standing by his feet.

The closest figure looked busy, turning this way and that, handling things, perhaps implements.

'I felt naked at the time,' recalled Mik. 'I didn't feel cold, but I could feel a draught on the whole of my body. My head and my arms were restrained, so I couldn't move, my body felt numb.

'I seem to remember them cutting me and scraping and digging, but I didn't feel any pain.'

Still groggy, Mik screwed up his eyes to try to make sense of the flashing colours that flickered on and off before him. He counted four rows of lights on what may have been a console.

The brightest light shone down from directly above him. 'It was like being in the dentist's when they look in your mouth,' recalled Mik. But this time he couldn't see who was doing the looking.

All he could see was the brown material of the cowls worn by the figures standing by his bed.

Then Mik was back face down, lying at the side of the football pitch, a raging headache pounding relentlessly.

Hauling himself to his feet he trudged over to his school pals. They believed he had gone to see the headteacher for treatment and wanted to know what he had said to him. 'I haven't been in school yet,' said Mik. His friends didn't believe him. They had been looking for him for fifteen minutes. He had disappeared from the spot at the side of the pitch where they had left him.

Mik went to the changing room to get out of his football strip and immediately noticed a red mark on his side. It hadn't been there earlier . . . but it was a scar that would remain with him for the rest of life.

Now in his late twenties, lorry driver Mik's entire life has been plagued with odd experiences.

As a four year old he would tell his parents about the strange little girl who would come to visit him in his bedroom.

The vision, a little girl with her ginger hair tied back, would appear behind the convector heater in a corner of his room. The youngster would wake in the middle of the night screaming.

'I remember I wasn't scared of the little girl,' recalls Mik. 'I was scared of whatever it was that seemed to frighten her. You could tell she was scared by the look on her face.'

An elderly neighbour solved the riddle of the midnight visitor. She said the description the boy gave was of a little girl who had lived and died at the house some years before.

The child had been epileptic and was often locked away in her bedroom by a cruel stepmother. According to the story, one day the little girl suffered a fit and choked to death. Her body was found by the fire.

Later in life Mik had another gloomy vision. But this time it was a bizarre case of precognition. For two and a half years he was toubled by baffling visions.

'I seemed to be in the back of a church, dimly lit, lights at the front. There was something high to my right and a row of flashing lights. I could see a dim light ahead and walked along towards it. Then I saw somebody slumped over so I looked and he turned towards me. The right side of his face was missing . . . and the rest of the face was me.'

That was similar to the sight that greeted a traffic policeman when he arrived at the scene of a collision between a lorry being driven by Mik and a huge crane.

Explained Mik: 'The policeman pulled in behind my trailer and walked along the side on the grass verge. It would have been dark with the headlights of my lorry reflecting ahead like in my vision. The trailer would stand high at one side.

'The policeman would have walked upto the front and would have seen me hanging out of the front end of my cab. I turned to look at him and the right side of my face was hanging off.

'It's the only way I can describe it. I saw what he saw, only I saw it two years before it happened.'

Mik's is a not an untypical case – a UFO witness and possible abductee with a rich history of psychic and precognitive experiences.

A level-headed Northerner he never tries to embellish his accounts, and investigators who have spent some considerable time with him are convinced he is telling the truth.

Does this case support the school of thought that individuals who are sensitive to psychic events are often sensitive to UFO activity? Does this theory suggest that only a certain type of person will experience abduction phenomenon?

And does that mean that alien abduction is nothing more than a psychological phenomenon?

CLOSE ENCOUNTERS OF A SEXUAL KIND

Sex and abduction phenomenon may seem like odd companions, but it is an aspect of the abduction mystery that deserves close scrutiny. Earlier we pointed out the fact that strange abductions seem to have occurred throughout history with accounts abounding in ancient mythology and folk tales. Sex actually played a major part in many of those old stories, in fact in some cases it seemed to be the sole reason for the abduction.

Greek mythology tells of handsome Gods coupling with mortal maidens, sometimes inseminating them with their heavenly seed. Across the world similar stories can be found in plentiful supply.

Human sexuality and reproduction is a central part of all human cultures, naturally. It is the method by which humanity continues to exist. Reproduction is a prime directive from nature. The order to 'Go forth and multiply' was given to man, and maybe to others.

Having said that it could be argued that it is equally quite natural that the modern 'folklore' of alien abduction should have borrowed one of the most compelling ingredients from religion and mythology — sex. After all, abductees and the people who investigate abductions are human. And sex is one of the most powerful of human drives.

So where exactly does sex come in the abduction equation?

Right at the beginning.

The Betty and Barney Hill case, possibly the first recorded abduction, had strong indications of an alien interest in sex and reproduction. Betty underwent what can only be described as a gynaecological examination and was tested for pregnancy and Barney had sperm removed.

Indeed in the majority of cases that have followed there seems to be a strong interest by the 'visitors' in the human reproductive system.

Female abductees often describe how 'aliens' show particular interest in their sexual and reproductive organs when under examination. Males too also testify that their genitalia are often carefully scrutinised when being examined by their abductors. One South American abductee described how he was sexually aroused so his alien captors could gather samples of his semen.

Many female abduction victims report gynaecological problems following their encounters, the most common being an interruption in their menstruation. And some report rape or even sexual intercourse with their abductors.

Male abductees too have also gone on record saying that they had sexual intercourse with female aliens. But, once again, as we find with most abduction cases, the majority are from other parts of the world, largely the USA and South America.

As this book is concentrating on abduction phenomenon in Britain we will scrutinise three accounts from this country, all involving women. These are not the only known British cases involving claims of sexual activity between alleged aliens and humans, but they are all accepted as possible abductees by the British UFO Research Association. Their accounts have a very strong sexual-reproductive theme running through them – and above all they have been prepared to talk about this most sensitive of matters.

One of the women believes she had sex with an alien, another is convinced she was raped and the third had gynaecological problems which suggests that her reproductive system was tampered with.

The two women who claim that aliens had sex with them are unable to give graphic descriptions of those events because of the traumatic effect of their experiences. But reports like theirs have led researchers to ask whether abductions are carried out by different races of aliens. One of the reasons for this is that according to reports on the alien beings known as 'greys' – the slight grey-skinned entities with large eyes, thin mouth and almost non-existent nose – there is no evidence of external genitalia.

One pathology report on the evidence read: 'No apparent reproductive organs. Perhaps atrophied by evolutionary degeneration. No genitalia. In my judgement the absence of sexual organs suggests that some of the aliens, and perhaps all, do not produce in the same manner as Homo sapiens, that some of the bodies studied are produced perhaps by a system of cloning.'

So if the 'greys' were not responsible for our female victims of alien molestation, who was?

But before we look at these amazing cases in detail let us first consider some of the many theories that might provide some explanation for these close encounters of a sexual kind.

'A preoccupation with reproduction is a common theme from the earliest abductions onward, and a few stories describe rape, sexual activity and events that might be described as artificial insemination,' said Thomas E. Bullard after looking at the evidence available.

One theory is that alien sexual activity with humans has been going on for thousands of years. It may be a way of introducing new genes and new traits into the human race, some sort of genetic control. This body of opinion states that a benign advanced alien culture could be using a form of super genetics to keep our race on the straight and narrow, ensuring a steady rate of development.

The other side of the coin portrays an alien Big Brother with a firm grip on our genetic reins ensuring we develop at the rate and level that suits them.

Another theory, popular in America, is that aliens are involved in the harvesting of genetic material for the continuation of their own kind. If an advanced extra-terrestrial culture has evolved down some genetic cul-de-sac, is it not possible that they may need to reinvigorate their stock of genes?

If they come across a race whose physical make-up is not so different from theirs might they take the opportunity of 'borrowing' some new genetic material?

The 'strange harvest' school of thought points to the controversial mutilation of livestock in the USA and says that the removal of sex organs with surgical precision from these animals could be another sign of an alien search for answers to a genetic nightmare we can't imagine.

But why bother with genetic experimentation when the earth is full of women capable of being used as surrogates for the procreation of an alien race.

For a number of years many female abductees have complained of alleged missing pregnancies defined as 'Missing Embryo/Foetus Syndrome'.

The women are pregnant, then after between six and twelve weeks their pregnancy simply stops. They have no sign of a miscarriage, have certainly not had an abortion, so where did their baby go?

A growing number of Ufologists in America believe these missing pregnancies are due to alien intervention. They believe suitable women are impregnated during abduction and then released only to be abducted again when the developing foetus can be removed.

New York Ufologist Budd Hopkins makes no bones about it. Some women, he alleges, are impregnated by aliens, have the resultant foetus removed to be brought to term elsewhere. He is convinced many women are being exploited as breeding stock.

He also points to the number of women who report 'wise baby dreams'. These women may have been through the missing pregnancy syndrome and follow up with dreams in which they see their babies intelligent . . . and alien.

So is abduction of our race being used to overcome the inability of some alien race to procreate?

'Highly unlikely,' is the response of many mainstream scientists. But how would they know the values and capabilities of a race so advanced that they have conquered star travel?

American psychotherapist Dr Jean Mundy is clear on alien genetic experimentation. She says: 'We don't know the full scale of the programme, only that it exists.

'Around nine per cent of women who claim alien contact report the disappearance (usually in the fourth month) of medically confirmed pregnancies. No evidence of miscarriage was found; they simply stopped being pregnant.

'Some of these women wondered if the aliens are using them as surrogate mothers.'

Could sperm be taken from male abductees and be used to

fertilise alien eggs to provide a further supply of crossbreeds? The permutations are endless.

American Air Force pilot John Lear added to this debate when he claimed a secret US Government body had made an agreement with a species of aliens known as EBEs, Extra-terrestrial Biological Entities, to ignore human abductions and mutilations of animals in return for high technology data.

Human and animal genetic material was essential for the EBE's survival, it was claimed.

There is a mass of so-called evidence in the hands of Ufologists in the United States, some in the form of alleged top secret Government papers dictated for the information of the President. These documents, which are steeped in contro-versy, suggest contact between alien entities and Govern-ment bodies over a long period of time and contain pages of information on the visitors.

Interestingly one of these papers discusses alien manipula-tion of DNA – the genetic building blocks of life – in terrestrial primates over a period of 25,000 years.

Are we laboratory rats in a bizarre alien experiment? Does planet Earth offer a battery of surrogate mums to help top up an infertile race of ETs with a new supply of crossbreeds? Or is the sexual aspect of abduction phenomenon simply a matter of Freudian theory surfacing in a psychotic experience?

The following cases should give you plenty to think about.

Lynda Jones,
19 August 1979,
Didsbury,
Greater Manchester.

The summer morning got off to a good start for thirty six year old housewife and mother of two Lynda Jones when a very old friend called at the comfortable semi-detached home she shared with husband Trevor and their two children Andrew, five and fifteen year old Dawn.

Over a long, leisurely lunch they chatted about the good old days and long lost acquaintances until Trevor had to leave for work at a nearby factory.

Trevor was on a 2 p.m. till 10 p.m. shift and left his wife and their mutual friend to while away the afternoon in the sundrenched garden watching the children at play.

The hours slipped by as Lynda and the family friend lounged in the baking heat of the day reminiscing about days gone by.

'Suddenly it was early evening and our friend reminded me he had to be on his way before lighting up time,' recalled Lynda. 'He had cycled over to see us on an old bike which had no lights.

'I said we would show him a short-cut over the fields. It would be nice to take a walk with the children and I could indulge my passion for wild flowers.'

It was about 7.30 p.m. when Lynda, the family friend, pushing his bike, and the children set off over the fields that border the River Mersey which meanders through this southern part of the Greater Manchester conurbation. The Jones family would accompany him as far as Simon's Bridge, a fifteen minute walk across the high grassland, and then wander back home at their leisure.

After saying their goodbyes, Lynda, clutching her copy of The Oxford Dictionary of Wildflowers, began hunting for the colourful plants that were now her hobby.

The three of them ambled through the grass, Lynda and Dawn often stopping to inspect an intriguing looking flower or plant, while young Andrew raced this way and that, relishing the freedom of the open countryside. They were in no hurry.

Trevor would not be home for a couple of hours yet. So they could zig-zag back across the fields at their leisure.

Suddenly Dawn called: 'Mum, the Moon is coming towards us.'

Lynda looked up to see a strange object racing across the sky, and apparently on a collision course with them.

'It was like a frisbee only a lot bigger,' remembers Lynda. 'It had come into view from behind some trees on the golf course on the other side of the river and I could see a few golfers on the green as it came towards us. It was no optical illusion.

'The object had a spinning effect and it seemed to be coming at us at an angle.'

'Get down,' Lynda ordered. 'Come on, get down in the grass.'

It was a natural instinct to hide in the tall grass. For one fleeting instant Lynda thought the object might be a plane from nearby Manchester Airport, perhaps it was in trouble, or on fire. She feared it might crash.

As she crouched down in the undergrowth, an arm around each of her children, Lynda braced herself for an explosion, the sound of an aircraft coming to earth nearby. But there was nothing, only silence.

Slowly raising her head above the grass, Lynda saw the object pass overhead and then drop vertically and silently behind an embankment, part of the river's flooding defences.

That's when the total silence that now surrounded her hit home. 'It was more than just silence, it was a complete stillness,' Lynda recalled later. 'There had been no noise from the object and then I realised there was no other noise either. No birdsong and no traffic noise from the nearby motorway.

'The traffic normally provides a constant background noise day and night because it is so busy. But at that moment it had gone completely.'

Pulling her children from the grass, Lynda took a few steps towards the embankment behind which the object had landed. Maybe it had crashed and the embankment was hiding wreckage. Perhaps it was on fire.

Whatever, Lynda had a compelling urge to get closer to the

object, and began walking and then running to the top of the embankment determined to see what it was hiding. As she reached the edge she had to catch her breath in shock at the sheer strangeness of the sight that greeted her eyes.

There, about thirty yards away on the bank of the river, lay an object which she could only describe as 'biblical'.

'That was the first word that popped into my head when I looked at it,' recalled Lynda. 'It was just so weird. I did not know anything about UFOs, I just wasn't interested in that sort of thing, but looking back what I saw did not fit the standard description of a flying saucer or a UFO.

'It was shaped like a crescent moon and coloured dark grey, but not metallic. It was made of a sort of lattice-work, an intricate design of lattice-work, but I could still see the field through it.

'It looked so, so old fashioned. It really did look like something out of the Bible.'

With her children standing beside her Lynda stared at the object, almost unable to take her eyes away, as she took in every detail.

'I would say it was about sixty feet across and was hovering perhaps two feet off the ground.

'Somehow, while we were watching it, it seemed to disappear, then appear and then disappear again.

'It had this light on the top of it, a bright white light that was separated from the structure beneath yet was still a part of it. I felt really drawn to it. As I stepped forward the light began to get brighter and brighter the nearer I got.'

As she edged her way towards the confusing shape before her, Lynda saw an orange ball of light appear from the far side of the object and begin to move towards her, rotating slowly.

'As I walked on towards the object I thought that in a few moments I would be looking in at them and what they were doing,' said Lynda. 'I don't know why I thought that but now it gives me the shivers.'

Suddenly Dawn screamed: 'Mum, come back. Come back . . .'

The fear in her daughter's voice jolted Lynda back to a terrifying reality.

'I had this feeling of deja vu, really strongly. Then I took in everything around me and I thought 'Oh my God. This is Judgement Day . . . I'm not ready for this.'

Lynda turned and fled. Grabbing her children by their hands, she charged back down the embankment, gripped with fear, heart pounding and eyes firmly focused on her escape route . . .

Running down the slope they quickly picked up speed. Only little Andrew faltered and struggled to keep up with the headlong pace of his panic-stricken mum and older sister.

'It's there again, the thing is back at the side of us,' screamed Dawn. Lynda's blood seemed to turn to ice in her veins. Too terrified to look back, she scooped up young Andrew before his tired five year old legs could give way under him, tightened her grip on her daughter's hand and drawing on every ounce of strength in her body she powered off through the grassland as if pursued by the devil himself.

As if in slow-motion Lynda forced one exhausted leg before the other in long, loping strides that carried her and her little son across the grassy terrain at the same breakneck speed that her younger, fitter daughter had set.

'Mum, look. There are two of them now,' Dawn called. Breathless, sweating and on the very edge of exhaustion, Lynda suppressed the urge to turn to look at her pursuers, and with what seemed superhuman strength increased the pounding rhythm of her legs.

'Don't look back Dawn, just run,' she yelled as she leapt onto the path that ran along the river, glad of a smoother surface on which she could increase the distance between the ominous object and her family.

Little Andrew, too frightened to speak, clung precariously to his mother as she ran side by side with her daughter on the final leg of their nightmare flight from fear.

And she held the youngster closer to her than ever as the odd presence had a bizarre effect on their surroundings.

'It was so strange,' recalled Lynda.' The grass was folding down on itself, as if it was being pressed down from above. It happened as we reached the river path. The grass all along the side was just folding. It was the strangest sight I have ever seen.'

Lynda and her daughter maintained their punishing pace even when they reached the edge of the housing estate where they lived.

'We didn't stop running until we got into the house,' said Lynda. 'Then we ran straight into Trevor who looked at me and said 'What's wrong with your eyes?' I looked in the mirror and I could see my skin was red and scaly under both my eyes. Dawn and Andrew were both OK.

'I told Trevor what we had seen from start to finish. He wanted us all to draw a picture of what we had seen.'

Lynda's daughter had been so petrified by the experience that she had wet herself and needed to change. But later when Trevor studied the drawings of his wife and daughter he had to agree that they were similar.

Suddenly Lynda realised Trevor was home, yet he had been on a two till ten shift and would not normally get home until 10.30 p.m.

'What time is it?' she asked her husband. 'It's gone ten thirty,' he replied.

Lynda had 'lost' at least an hour of her life. She and the children had left their home for the walk at 7.30 p.m. They had seen the strange object at about 9 p.m. and had run the distance of a ten-minute walk at breakneck speed. Yet they didn't get in until 10.30 p.m.

Lynda would have to wait another eighteen months to discover more about her experience when she would undergo hypnosis. In the meantime she and Trevor told very few people of her encounter.

One friend, who had been told, called the Air Traffic Control at Manchester Airport to see if they could throw any light on the mystery. All they could say was that they had no air traffic which would match the object's 'Biblical' description!

In 1980 Lynda underwent a series of hypnotic regression sessions. Each session was recorded on videotape and produced ten hours of recordings in all. But Lynda found the entire experience disturbing and frightening and has refused to view the majority of the tapes.

She said: 'It was very unsettling watching myself under hypnosis. At times I was becoming extremely upset by whatever I thought was happening to me. It was just too much.'

However in the years since, Lynda has pieced together a vague yet intriguing account of what may have happened to her during that missing hour or so, based partially on memories re-awakened by hypnotic regression and other snatches of information that have surfaced over a period of time.

'I believe that at the point where the children and I turned to run away, I saw a person standing by the object. I was transfixed, unable to move, just as in a dream. Then I had a feeling of floating, as if I was moving unintentionally.

'Then I am in a room and six beings come in. They are like humans, wearing dark suits, like motorbike suits with high necks.

'The beings, or whatever they were, seemed Oriental. They had slanted eyes, very dark hair and yellow/olive skins.

'I seemed to know one of them, as if I had seen him before.

'Then I felt as if I was being examined. I felt as if I was laid down on a table in this strange room and they were examining me. I distinctly remember them putting something on my legs; it felt like they were putting pieces of ice on me. Every time I turned my head to look at what they were doing, bright lights were shone in my eyes'

Lynda still finds the memories of that evening's strange events frightening and refuses to speculate about what was being done to her on that examination table.

But the real-life medical side-effects she has suffered ever since her encounter make her quake with fear.

Lynda, like many other female abduction victims, discovered that her menstrual cycle had been affected. Within a few weeks, she visited her GP to tell him her periods had stopped. He told her she had nothing to worry about, these things can happen.

'I knew I was too young to be on the change,' said Lynda. 'But I wasn't really worried.'

Lynda tried to get on with her life but suddenly found she was prone to strange marks appearing and then disappearing on her body.

'I'd get a mark, Trevor would see it but it would have gone by the time I got to the doctors. It was really strange,' said Lynda.

But the most mystifying after-effect came some weeks after

her encounter. She had been feeling tired and listless. Then one day she had what she describes as a 'show'.

'I feel terrible talking about something as personal as this,' she said. 'But this waxy material came away. I was really worried and took it to my GP. He took one look at it and said 'You've had a miscarriage.'

'But I had not been pregnant,' said Lynda. 'I was stunned.'

Lynda's menstruation did not return and she was referred by her GP to a gynaecologist who embarked on a long series of tests and examinations to get help with her problem.

After a time Lynda was called into hospital to see her specialist. He had found something.

'They had looked at my Fallopian tubes and found some scar tissue on them. They said that type of scarring could only have been caused by an ectopic pregnancy, where the egg is fertilised and develops in the Fallopian tube.'

'But I had never had an ectopic pregnancy to my knowledge. I would have known because an ectopic pregnancy can be fatal.'

Was Lynda conscripted into an alien genetic-testing culture? Budd Hopkins would certainly consider Lynda's case as supporting his worrying theories.

As he recently said: 'What we get is an alien concentrating on taking samples and working on the reproductive area without the abductee's will being involved.'

But Lynda does not feel qualified to speculate. She said:' I don't know what happened to me, but something did. To be honest it frightens me. It has made me look at lots of other events in my life and wonder.'

Immediately after her experience she noticed a strange mark on the jeans that she had been wearing when she crossed the field. Amazingly it was in the shape of the object she saw and even matched the drawings she and her daughter had done of the object.

'The jeans were tested at a university institute. They said that the image could have been done with printer's ink, but why in that shape?' asked Lynda.

Seven years later Lynda was working as a beauty consultant and was asked to wear a plastic name badge. Her name disappeared from the badge within hours. The same happened with a further two badges issued to her.

'The badges were again tested by a scientist, who said it could have something to do with radio waves,' said a perplexed Lynda.

But above all the encounter, the strange after-effects made Lynda re-evaluate other odd events that she had buried away.

'Trevor and I experienced a missing time episode in 1972,' said Lynda. 'We went out for a spin in his E-type Jaguar. We took the country roads through Cheshire. It was early evening and we planned to go for a drink.'

Trevor came to a halt by some traffic lights. He suggested he and Lynda call in for a drink at the pub at the next corner. It was about 9 p.m. Suddenly the car began to spin.

'One minute we were sitting there, the next the car was going round and round. Trevor had the hand brake on and his foot jammed on the brake, but the car just spun as if on ice,' remembered Lynda.

'Trevor asked me if I could see some bright lights behind us. Then the car stopped and he pulled away and turned left at the pub.'

'We didn't get out of the car because we could see the pub was closed so we drove home.'

'But when we got home it was 3 a.m. Somehow we had lost six hours.'

Some observers would say that Lynda's experiences are similar to those of alleged abductees, particularly in America, who, it is claimed are chosen for genetic experimentation by alien visitors.

Some Ufologists maintain these individuals are abducted and tested and re-abducted again and again to glean further information, like zoologists or biologists who capture and tag wild animals only to release them and recapture them to monitor their progress and development.

Lynda's view? 'I don't understand what has happened to me. It is all very weird. I wish someone could explain it to me.'

Gabriella Versacci (pseudonym),
16 October 1973,
Langford Budville,
Somerset.

Gabriella Versacci was making spaghetti for her husband Alberto and their fourteen year old daughter Maria when a sharp rap at the front door made her jump. The thirty three year old housewife turned down the heat on the stove and padded out to the door to find the daughter of her friend on the doorstep.

"Hello Gabriella, my mum asked me to call to see if you could drive over to Wellington to see her, she's not very well at the moment," said the young woman.

"Of course, of course it is no problem," soothed Gabriella. In the ten years since she and her husband had landed in Britain from their native Turin she had made many friends. "In a new country we must make new friends," her husband Alberto always said and Gabriella's warm and helpful nature meant she was always in great demand.

"I'm in the middle of making the evening meal," she told her young visitor. "Give me half an hour and I'll drive over."

That promise was a little optimistic. Minutes after her friend's daughter had left there was someone else at the door.

A stream of visitors seemed to call at the Versacci's Taunton home that night and Gabriella didn't have the heart to turn anybody away, so it was well after 10.30 p.m. when Gabriella climbed into her 1967 Mini Saloon for the drive to Wellington.

Determined to make up for lost time, Gabriella decided to avoid Taunton town centre and took the A361 to Milverton where she would take the B3187 to Wellington itself. Despite the light traffic it was about 11.30 p.m. when she turned into the small, winding B-road which snaked across country to her destination.

As she passed the Langford Budville signpost, about three miles from Wellington, Gabriella could see the road was completely deserted.

Then as she wound along the country lane she thought she

saw the glare of a single headlight ahead. As her car bowled along the clear road she realised the light ahead was too bright to be a headlight and it seemed stationary.

'Strange,' she thought, 'there are no buildings at that spot.'

Concentrating on her driving, she pressed on in the hope that her friend would not object to such a late visitor. She had promised her daughter that she would pay her sick friend a visit and a promise was a promise.

Suddenly the car seemed to lose power. The headlamps flickered, dimmed and then cut out. Next the engine faltered, spluttered and then fell silent. Panic-stricken, Gabriella pressed her face to the windscreen, struggling to steer the car to a halt in the almost complete blackness.

When the Mini came to a standstill by the side of the road, Gabriella put on the handbrake, knocked the gearstick into neutral and turned the key in the ignition. Nothing.

Nervously she glanced over to the bright light she had seen from the road earlier. Had that got anything to do with her breakdown? For some reason she felt sure it had.

Pulling herself together, Gabriella tried the ignition again. But the electrics were obviously dead.

Sitting alone in a silent car on a deserted country road and enveloped by complete darkness, the fear began to well up inside her. Gabriella decided she couldn't sit there and do nothing.

Even if she didn't know what she was doing she ought to look under the bonnet. It might be something simple like a loose wire. She climbed out of the claustrophobic confines of her little car. At least she would be doing something.

Out in the night Gabriella fumbled with the bonnet catch and lifted it. In the gloom she peered at, what to her, was merely a jumble of oddly-shaped parts. As she stood there helplessly, she noticed a humming sound, faint at first then seeming to grow stronger.

Raising her head from beneath the bonnet, she glanced over at the strange bright light and became aware that the noise wasn't coming from any particular direction. It was the regular hum of an electricity generator and seemed to lie like a blanket over the whole area.

Closing the bonnet, Gabriella decided she would try the

ignition once again. Whatever the fault was, maybe it was OK now, she thought as she tugged on the driver door.

A hand came down on her left shoulder. A heavy hand seemingly pushing her down into the ground. Turning slowly, trying to keep at bay the sense of panic that threatened to turn her into a gibbering wreck, Gabriella faced her assailant. He was tall, dark-coloured and metallic.

'Robot', the word crashed around her brain. Gabriella was being waylaid by a metal man. He was certainly more machine than man by the way the light from the bright object in the field was reflected off his metallic surface. Then more lights – flashing, coloured lights – and then all was blackness for Gabriella Versacci.

When she came to from her fear-induced faint, Gabriella was standing in a field. The robot was next to her and before them stood the strange, bright object. Half-moon shaped, it was rounded at the top and flat at the bottom.

Bright as an arc lamp, the object was some sort of machine. This impression became stronger as the brightness emitted by the object was reduced. It was silver-grey in colour, not unlike aluminium. It rested on thick legs, Gabriella saw two but there may have been more.

Transfixed to the spot, Gabriella's eyes explored the object for clues to its purpose. It was about twenty feet high and forty feet across. Large, oblong windows punctuated its middle and from these a yellow light issued.

Now Gabriella realised it was the object that was emitting the humming sound. With that realisation the overwhelmed housewife blacked out for the second time that night.

She awoke inside a strange room, which she took to be the interior of the object. She found herself in a circular room, strapped to a table in the centre. Naked, Gabriella wondered who had undressed her. She was grateful for the large light blue blanket that covered her embarrassment.

Gabriella tried in vain to raise herself for a better look at her 'prison'. Her wrists were bound to the table by what she described as 'large rubber bands'. Her spread-eagled legs were restrained in the same manner, with the bands holding her ankles to the cold surface of the table.

Gabriella shivered. The blue blanket was cold and the

inside of the craft was freezing. She glanced over to a far wall where the 'robot' stood inactive. The wall behind him was covered with an array of equipment. To Gabriella's right was a console covered in buttons and dials.

She looked down and saw the floor was covered in what looked like a black coloured rubber matting.

Although she couldn't see directly behind her, Gabriella felt that was where the entrance to the room lay. She was proved right a few moments later when three men came into view. Two stood to the left of the table while the third went to the foot of the table and picked up some boxes, or cubes.

He placed three of the objects on a rail which ran the length of the table, one by her head, one by her feet and one in the middle. As soon as the cubes were placed on the rail they began to glow

Gabriella studied the three men, all of whom were about the same height, five feet six inches or five feet eight inches. Fair-skinned and slim in build they wore the same garments. All wore a skull cap, tied at the back of the head and ending just above the eyes. Face masks covered the nose and mouth, so only the eyes and facial parts around them were visible to Gabriella.

No hair was visible, but she could make out the hair bumps under the caps.

The eyes, more rounded than human eyes, seemed emotionless.

All three men wore a tunic with a grey-coloured edging, long gloves that went to the elbows and very long aprons that fell as far as their ankles. Thick-soled boots covered their feet. Every piece of clothing was the same colour – light blue.

Throughout the episode, none of Gabriella's captors either spoke or made any other noise. They looked at each other frequently, and nodded occasionally. Furthermore they didn't appear to breathe, making no respiratory noises

During the examination none of the three beings touched Gabriella. The examiner, the man at the bottom of the bed, took a number of grey-coloured instruments, which he used one by one. A small knife-like implement, was used to take a nail paring from her right hand index finger. A blood sample was taken with a small plastic-looking bottle with tubes and wires attached. A small device, which he held in the palm of his hand, was passed over the body and glowed with varying degrees of brightness depending on its location over Gabriella's body.

At one stage the examiner removed the blue blanket leaving her cold and embarrassed.

A thin pencil-like device was used to prod and probe her and a large black rubber suction device was used on the area around her groin. Pushed firmly onto the skin and lifted again, this caused some discomfort for Gabriella, although the rest of the process was totally painless.

Shivering badly at one stage, the examiner placed another blanket over her which provided badly needed extra warmth. Gabriella deemed the examination over when the man pulled the new black blanket over her entire body.

Noticing her frequent glances towards the now inactive robot the examiner spoke to her in perfect English.

The robot was a trained retriever device, he said. It did all the manual work outside the ship. It brought specimens for examination and study. It was merely a non-thinking intelligence that was programmed to do certain tasks. The examiner spoke with a deep male voice, although Gabriella could not see his mouth move beneath his mask.

The examiner then removed the three glowing tubes from the rail. As he worked she noticed he had five digits on each hand; every movement looked practised, deliberate and precise. His eyes never blinked, not even once.

When he completed his task, all three men left the room together.

For several minutes Gabriella lay there. Further attempts to move were thwarted by the rubber bands at her wrists and ankles. When she tried to scream she found her throat too sore and painful. Once she tried to vomit and couldn't.

She caught site of the robot again. A flashing purple-coloured light coming from it. It did not move but remained by the wall.

Gabriella's attention was caught by a movement behind her. One of the three men came into view from behind her and walked to the far end of the table.

He lifted the end of the blanket from the bottom and stared

at her body. There was still no visible emotion in his eyes. The being stood, with the end of the blanket in one hand, his eyes boring into her.

Frightened, Gabriella sensed something horrible was about to happen. She struggled with her bonds frantically, but it was no good. The strong bands held her firmly to the table. The being took a small pin and placed it on her thigh. Gabriella stopped struggling immediately. The device caused a semi-paralysis, numbing everything apart from her head.

Rocking her head from side to side, Gabriella tried to scream, but her throat was too dry and sore. She tried to cry, but even that release was denied her.

The being climbed slowly on to the bottom of the bed.

'Oh my God,' she thought. 'He is raping me.'

Gabriella didn't look, and couldn't move during the cold, calculating act of depravity.

But she felt the being's every move. Praying to God for release, she felt sick at his cold alien touch. But there was nothing she could do. The paralysis prevented her from fighting back.

Feeling great discomfort, but no pain, Gabriella's mind drifted back to her sick friend in Wellington, her husband and her daughter. What would they think if they knew of this she thought to herself.

When the man had finished he slowly climbed off the table, pulled down the black blanket to totally cover her body and left the room.

Alone once again Gabriella became almost hysterical at the implications of what had just happened. She was not aware of the alien having had an emission but nevertheless she realised it was not beyond possibility that she might become pregnant. Would the child be an alien? How would she tell her husband?

The three men came into the room again, one removed the pin device from her thigh, while the other two lifted the blanket, folded it and placed it neatly on the floor by the console.

They removed the bands from her wrists and ankles and lifted her off the table.

Gabriella looked down to see her clothes on the floor by the robot before passing out for the third time that night

When she next gained consciousness Gabriella was standing, fully clothed, next to her car in the deserted country road. Dazed and shocked, she climbed in the vehicle, turned the key in the ignition and to her surprise the engine started first time.

Gabriella did not remember the journey home. In a state of acute shock and looking ruffled and extremely upset she walked into her house at 2.30 a.m. An anxious Alberto held his distraught wife as she told him her sorry tale.

That night the Versacci's made a pact never to relate the story to anyone else. They would simply try to pick up the pieces and try to get on with their lives.

Four years later, the Versaccis had managed to keep Gabriella's encounter out of the public eye, but hungry for knowledge she approached a UFO investigator who set about researching her case.

His verdict? Gabriella Versacci had nothing to gain and much to lose by seeking help over her encounter. She was found to be honest and trustworthy and her account consistent with many similar cases. In fact she was so concerned about the possible after-effects of the rape that she took a pregnancy test shortly afterwards. It proved negative.

Investigators noticed a series of amazing similarities between the Versacci case and that of police chief Jeff Greenhaw in the United States. His encounter came just one day after Gabriella's and the similarities between a 'robot' he describes and the 'robot' like-figure which apprehended the British housewife appear too much for coincidence.

At about 10 p.m. on the night of 17 October 1973, twenty six year old Greenhaw was the only full-time police officer in the town of Falkville, Alabama.

He was off-duty and at home when a woman called in to say she had just seen a UFO with flashing lights land in a field to the west of the town. After a recent spate of sightings, Greenhaw picked up his camera and sped off in the direction of the reported sighting.

When he arrived at the location he made contact with the mystery intruder almost immediately. Standing in the middle of the road, it was wearing a silver suit, like tinfoil, said Greenhaw in his report.

He said the figure seemed tall and had something like an antenna on its head. After he had faced the entity for a few moments it began to approach him at which the police officer fired off four shots using a flash. The pictures, although blurred, show a figure moving towards the frightened officer.

Greenhaw raced to his patrol car and switched on the revolving light on its roof. The resulting flash of lights and noise of the siren caused the figure to turn and flee.

Greenhaw claims to have given chase, but said the figure escaped at high speed over the rough gravelly road.

'He was running faster than any human I ever saw,' said the policeman.

Greenhaw's much-publicised case may have given him instant fame. But it cost him his marriage (his wife abhorred the notoriety), his home, which burned down mysteriously, and his job. His police bosses thought his involvement with UFOs had damaged his credibility as a police officer.

The case was also tarnished by the suggestion that Greenhaw was involved in a hoax.

However it would have been impossible for Mrs Versacci to have based her description of the robot in her encounter on the Greenhaw case. She had no known links to Ufology society, outside of which the American case is virtually unknown. And she gave her description of the robot-like figure who 'captured' her to her husband BEFORE the Greenhaw case occurred.

Investigators also agree that Mrs Versacci, a private woman, a respectable housewife and mother, would have no motive to concoct such an encounter story, particularly one in which she was the victim of a sexual assault of the most serious kind.

A religious woman, she was deeply affected by the alleged attack and to this day has refused to allow her real name to be connected to the report.

Jane Murphy,
March 1981,
Birstall,
West Yorkshire.

Jane Murphy was asleep the minute her head hit the pillow. For the twenty two year old housewife and mum of a baby daughter it had been another exhausting day. Husband Mick had climbed into bed as Jane tucked little Sharon cosily in her cot. She only just had the strength to get undressed and slip her nightie over her head before sliding between the covers.

But the sleep ended as quickly as it had come. Jane was awake but kept her eyes closed. For some reason she couldn't hear Mick's snores and the feel of the room was all wrong.

When she opened her eyes Jane was standing in a field. She could feel the grass beneath her feet and looked up at a night sky heavy with cloud. It was cold but not uncomfortably so.

'I knew where I was,' remembers Jane. 'But I wasn't sure how I'd got there. I had the feeling that I had been led there to this field near to where my mum lives. There was a farm I recognised but there was something over to one side that I hadn't seen before.'

The object hovering over the field was huge and metallic but Jane did not have time to study it. Her attention was caught by the movement of a group of figures, perhaps as many as ten.

The figures were vaguely humanoid, but for some reason Jane could not focus on them.

'They were just coming towards me,' said Jane. 'One had a mask or a cloth in his hand and put it over my nose and mouth. I seemed to know they wanted to put me out so I pretended to be unconscious.

'But that didn't work. They seemed to know I was awake and two of them held me and one gave me some sort of injection. I assumed it was an injection because I felt the prick.'

Jane blacked out.

When she came round the working class Yorkshire girl assumed she had been taken into the strange object by the 'men' who had captured her.

'When I woke up I was on my hands and knees on this table in a strange room and I was really frightened. I just buried my head in my hands because I didn't want to look,' recalled Jane. 'I knew the figures were there but I didn't want to see them. Then they kept telling me to look at them. They weren't speaking, the words just came into my mind.'

Fighting back the fear, Jane forced herself to look at her captors. The entity she faced was very tall, nearly seven feet, and human looking. Then Jane saw his eyes.

'They were black, totally black,' she said. 'Apart from that I would have said he was human. He wasn't a monster by any means.'

The young woman was then told she must bathe and they indicated a plastic looking object that looked nothing like a tub. Obediently Jane slipped off her nightie and sat in the 'bath'.

'It just fitted around me, it was the same shape as my body, as if it was made for me,' said Jane. 'It didn't have any water in it but I went through the motions of washing and when I got out I was clean.'

Jane was helped back on to the table in the centre of the room and now noticed that all but one of the humanoid figures had gone. The tall man who she had seen first remained with her.

Slowly the being moved towards Jane, bringing his face close to hers.

'I just looked into his big black eyes and knew that it was going to happen,' recalls Jane.

'Suddenly he was lying on the table and I was on top of him. We were sort of embracing, but lying very still. I remember noticing his smell. It wasn't very pleasant, not a human smell at all.

'Then we were having sex. It was the strangest sensation of all. We were lying together, not moving, but all the sensations of human sex were there. I looked at him, into his eyes and said "Why me?"

'The reply was strange because the idea came into my

mind that he was saying "Because we love you", but it was said coldly. There was no emotion there at all.

'I couldn't even tell you if he had any clothes on or not because I simply looked into his eyes. All I remember visually are those gigantic black eyes.

'I didn't think about it as a physical act. I can't say that I was conscious of his penis, because I wasn't, but inside, inside me it was all happening.'

'I believe I came to a climax because at the time I felt it was the best sex that I had ever had. It seemed so strange lying on top of this stranger, not moving yet having sex and enjoying it.'

After about five minutes Jane realised others had now entered the room. The newcomers included female humanoids. Her sex partner climbed off the table and left the room, while the remaining humanoids prepared Jane for an examination.

Some of the examiners appeared to use long instruments for what was obviously a gynaecological examination of the young human.

Jane felt no pain or major discomfort and, after the examination, was taken on a tour of the strange craft.

She was shown a table covered with a number of brightly coloured pills in geometric shapes. She was invited to try one and did so. But when she later tried to take a drink from a cup, an alien using a powerful telepathic message told her to stop.

'I don't remember much of my tour of the ship but I do remember seeing other humans,' she recalls.

Jane's visit ended as abruptly as it had begun.

She suddenly found herself back in bed, the alarm clock said it was 6.28 p.m., nearly time for Mick to set off for work.

Could it all have been a dream? Jane asked herself. Then she remembered the injection and looked at her arm. The skin was still slightly bruised around the tiny puncture mark made by the needle.

'I had a strong desire to bathe,' recalls Jane.' I remember thinking I must wash otherwise I would have that bad smell clinging to me, the alien smell.'

Then as she climbed into the bath Jane felt a heaviness in

Top Left: William Barrett at the scene of his encounter & holding a model of the object he observed. Courtesy of William Barrett
Top Right: Rosalind Reynolds. Courtesy of Albert Budden.
Above Left: Mik Burley at the wreck of the accident which he foresaw. Courtesy of Mik Burley.
Above Right: Rohan Hinton. Photograph courtesy of Rohan Hinton.

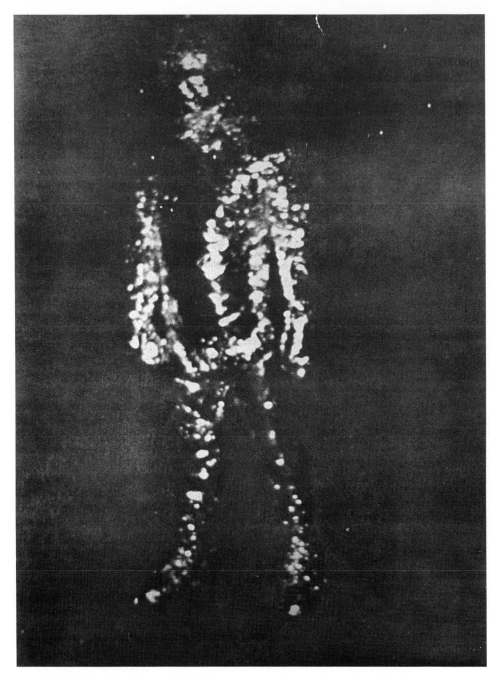

Above: Falkville, Alabama, 17th October 1973. Taken by Police Chief Jeff Greenshaw. Courtesy of Fortean Picture Library. The incident took place only a day apart from the Versacci case & the robots observed by Mrs Versacci were very similar to the entity photographed by Jeff Greenshaw.

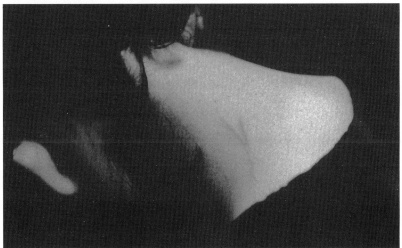

Top: Lynda Jones.
Middle: Scar on Jane Murphy's neck which appeared after one of her many close encounter experiences.
Above: Site of Jane Murphy's abduction experience.

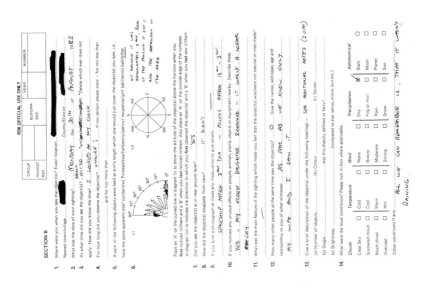

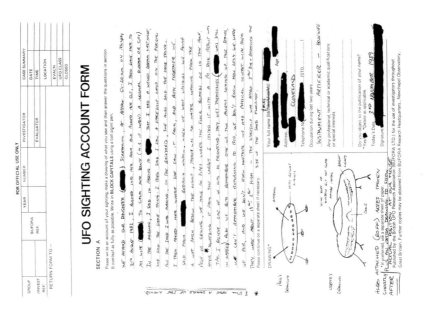

Top: *The original UFO sighting account form completed by George and Amanda Phillips for the British UFO Research Association (minus personal details.)*

her stomach, the sort of heaviness she remembered from pregnancy.

That sensation was the beginning of a series of odd events that followed her encounter.

First her menstrual cycle stopped completely, something which her doctor could not explain. Then she was referred to hospital for tests following her continued complaints about the heaviness in her stomach. Doctors gave her the all clear.

Finally she was plagued for three months with a vaginal complaint that doctors diagnosed as 'an infection'. Fearful that it may have been associated with the alien with whom she had sex, Jane tried one course of tablets after another without success. Once again her GP referred her to a hospital. This time a powerful course of antibiotics did the trick.

But although the medical after-effects of her encounter had now abated, Jane's life had changed beyond recognition. Within months her alien captors were back.

'They were here in the house,' explained Jane. 'I don't know how they got in, but there was a man and a woman. They were just like the people I saw on the craft.

They began pumping the girl for information, data. She must tell them all she knew.

'They wanted to know how babies were born,' said Jane. 'It was ridiculous. I told them. Everybody knew about babies I said. But they said their people didn't.'

That was just the beginning of a series of visitations that drove Jane to the edge of a nervous breakdown.

She would wake in the night to find one or more of the alien visitors standing by her bed or wake in the morning and somehow 'know' she had been somewhere else in the night.

Then the dreams started. Strange dreams about being pregnant and giving birth. All the dreams had an alien involvement and in one she dreamed of giving birth to a blond, black-eyed alien hybrid.

'I don't know if I was on the spaceship,' she said. 'But I had the baby and it was blond and had its eyes closed. Then I looked again and he opened his eyes and they were black, like the aliens.'

Jane's abduction and the stress of innumerable further

visits put a strain on her relationship with her husband. He told her he did not believe that she had experienced these events.

'At one stage I thought I was going mad,' said Jane. 'I didn't want these things to happen to me, but they did. I just wanted to be normal.'

In desperation Jane sought help from the family doctor. 'Are you an LSD user?' He asked. Jane gave up. She did not believe she was hallucinating, yet a drug induced hallucination was the only explanation that occurred to her GP.

In July 1987 Jane's local paper carried an article about the British UFO Research Association's UFO Hotline, a 24 hour telephone service for witnesses to report sightings.

It was her last chance, she thought, as she dialled the number and left her message on the answerphone.

Within days the association's director of investigations, Philip Mantle, became involved.

The series of interviews that followed were enough to convince investigators that Jane was not a hoaxer. There was an element of contamination in view of the fact that she had read a number of abduction books after her encounter, but not enough to enable her to fabricate the entire episode.

What stunned investigators was the sheer number of alleged alien visits Jane recorded since her abduction encounter, which they estimated at more than a hundred.

In fact they worked out that Jane had her first UFO experience when she was just sixteen years old. At the time Jane was living with her mother near Leeds. Lying in bed one night, she heard a loud whirring noise and watched as her room was flooded by a bright red light. The following day she heard radio reports about a spate of UFO sightings in the area and connected them with the strange experience in her bedroom.

But that was only a prelude to her alleged abduction and the many alleged follow-up visits.

'I've been taken away many times by the aliens,' recalls Jane. 'Out into the fields or sometimes for examinations. Then other times I've had the dreams of being pregnant and once giving birth to this baby that had blond hair and alien's eyes.'

Jane's accounts were so close to those of one of the witnesses in the Budd Hopkins book *Intruders* that British investigators liaised with the American researcher. He was interested in gathering as much detail as possible.

Jane's dream about giving birth was also reminiscent of the Wise Baby Dreams that Hopkins refers to in his works.

Psychologist Dr John Shaw studied the Jane Murphy case and made the following observation: 'The most predominant effect on Jane seems to be a strong feeling of incomprehension. As she says in her transcript, 'I'd like to know what they want from me and why it's been happening for all these years.'

'The human drive to make sense of one's experiences is being greatly frustrated in Jane's case. This is not helped by the fact that she is a fairly unreflective individual, not given to close examination, it would appear, of her emotional and cognitive reactions.

'Trying to make sense of strange happenings is not all that unusual an occurrance. However this cannot usually be done without skilled help. This case underlines the need for a special kind of victim support system, either self-help groups, or one-to-one counselling or therapy.

'People like Jane have a desperate need to release their fears and be helped to develop a cognitive framework by which to understand what has happened to them.

'Victims need not stay victims. They can become wise as a result of their traumas.'

Jane's visitations are less frequent today and she is less willing to talk about them.

'I can't understand it so I try to put it behind me,' she said.

EPILOGUE

What is your verdict? You have read a couple of dozen British abduction mysteries that have been judged worthy of investigation by one or other of the UFO research organisations so now you can decide whether it is fact or fantasy.

Are we being visited by advanced technologies from beyond the stars? Are they keeping a fatherly eye on a fledgling human race in an immense and immensly dangerous universe? Or are these alien visitors playing Big Brother, using our population like laboratory rats in a bizarre genetic experiment which condemns some human women to a lifetime of exploitation as breeding machines for a selfish race of aliens?

Maybe that is all just so much nonsense. Perhaps Albert Budden is right. Hallucinations caused by an allergic reaction to electro-magnetic fields and many other things are at the root of the many abduction cases that flood in every year, and abductees are a significant minority of the population who are sensitive to changes in the environment.

Then again, isn't it more likely that the whole phenomenon has its cause hidden away inside the complex structures of the human mind.

A psychological explanation for abduction phenomenon has become very unfashionable in view of the big bucks being made out of Ufology in the United States. Free enterprise and super hype have virtually made alien abduction a fact of life in the USA.

As one renowned British investigator told us recently: 'It has got to the stage that if you go to any big US UFO convention these days and come up with a theory that actually questions the existence of UFOs and aliens then you're likely to get branded a heretic.'

The truth about UFOs, flying saucers and alien abduction is anybody's guess. We are no further along the road to truth in this field than we were back in 1947 when the term flying saucer was born.

Maybe you will become the abductee who will be in a position to offer the world incontrovertible evidence of the existence of UFOs, aliens and alien abductions. On the other hand maybe you won't.

For those of you who may now have developed a taste for investigating abduction phenomenon, there is a mass of literature available to allow you to delve even deeper. And if you fancy trying your hand as a real investigator why not contact one of the organisations mentioned at the end of this book.

Without Consent was intended to address the phenomenon as far as British abductees and interested parties were concerned. We wanted to set the scene for the uninitiated, for those who have never felt UFOs and Ufology as subjects worthy of serious consideration.

There is an even greater mass of information from different parts of the world.The cases we have looked at are just the tip of an enormous iceberg. And the theories we have mentioned represent a fraction, albeit a representative sample, of the innumerable explanations for abduction phenomenon.

At the beginning of this book we described most abductees as ordinary, sensible, rational people who had experienced a most extraordinary event in their lives. We decided to invite each and every one of them to offer an explanation of their individual experiences.

Strikingly few of our witnesses have felt qualified to say what they think was responsible for their encounters. Elsie Oakensen has an idea it could have been a spiritual event, Gabriella Versacci is convinced she has met beings from outer space. But the vast majority prefer to keep open minds. Their search for an explanation for the inexplicable continues.

APPENDIX A

Information about BUFORA and sample questionnaire.

ABOUT UFOS

The modern study of unidentified flying object phenomena (UFOs) is commonly held to have started with the report of Kenneth Arnold. On Tuesday 24 June 1947 Arnold, a private pilot, reported "nine peculiar aircraft" near Mount Rainier, Washington State, USA. In fact there appear to have been many reports over the years before Arnold's report. In the UK there are reports of strange aerial phenomena back at least to the turn of the century.

There are many theories about the possible origins or nature of these phenomena including, amongst others, UFOs may be natural phenomena and UFOs may be advanced technology. BUFORA recognises that there are a number of explanatory hypotheses and does not advocate any particular theory.

ABOUT BUFORA

BUFORA was founded in 1962, as a federation of UFO groups throughout the UK. Many of these groups were formed in the 1950's. These included the British Flying Saucer Bureau, founded in 1952, which is believed to be the UK's oldest UFO group. In 1962 the group was known as the British UFO Association, changing its name in 1964 to the present British UFO Research Association. BUFORA became a company limited by guarantee in 1975. This means that in the event of BUFORA being wound up each members undertaking to cover any outstanding debts is limited to £1. BUFORA is registered under the Data Protection act, and amongst other things membership records are held on a computer database. (It is the policy of BUFORA **NOT** to release membership records to third parties.)

BUFORA is run entirely by volunteers, relying solely on its members to fund and carry out its investigation, research and educational activities. The day to day running of BUFORA is in the hands of a Council of Management drawn from the members.

Membership of BUFORA is open to all who support the aims of the association, and whose application is approved by the Council of Management.

AIMS OF BUFORA

The three aims of BUFORA are:

1. To encourage, promote and conduct unbiased scientific research of unidentified flying object (UFO) phenomena throughout the United Kingdom.

2. To collect and disseminate evidence and data relating to unidentified flying objects.

3. To co-ordinate UFO research throughout the United Kingdom and to co-operate with others engaged in such research throughout the world.

ACTIVITIES OF BUFORA

In pursuit of its aims, BUFORA supports an active investigation team, and a research team. The investigation team carries out on site field investigation of cases, whilst the research team gets involved in activities such as statistical research and technical support activities. These activities are backed up by a press cutting service and extensive libraries of case reports and published literature on UFO phenomena. The heads of both the investigation and research teams are members of the Council of Management of BUFORA. Both are assisted in organising the activities of their sections by advisory committees made of of members with a special interest in these activities.

BUFORA organises in London a programme of monthly lectures (September to June) on a variety of UFO related topics. Additionally regional meetings are held, and every other year BUFORA co-sponsors the International UFO Conference. Members receive free of charge, six issues per year, of its regular publication 'UFO Times', which carries details of investigated reports and results of research projects. BUFORA operates with British Telecom the 'UFOCALL' hotline, which carries information about reports and updates on events (phone 0898-12-1886; Note charge currently 48p per minute peak rate, 36p off peak)

In recent years BUFORA has established its international reputation by its investigation and research work, and a number of major publications. BUFORA is a founder, and the UK representative organisation of the International Committee for UFO Research. BUFORA is the publisher of the 'UFO Lexicon', which is an international glossary of UFO-related terms in ten languages. BUFORA is involved in a number of collaborative projects with other UFO groups throughout the UK and the rest of the world.

PUBLICATIONS OF BUFORA

In addition to 'UFO Times', BUFORA has published a number of booklets and papers on specific aspects of research and investigation (for example our Vehicle Interference Report and Investigator Handbook), or as in depth case studies of specific reports (eg The Livingston Encounter). BUFORA publishes 'UFO World', a series which is an annual review of UFO investigation and research throughout the world. Recent publications include 'UFOs 1947-1987' (published by Fortean Tomes [1987]), 'Fire in the Sky' (BUFORA [1989]) and 'Controversy of the Circles' (BUFORA [1989]).

Details of publications currently available can be obtained from the registered office (enclose S.A.E. please).

REGISTERED OFFICE

BUFORA Ltd, 16 Southway, Burgess Hill, Sussex RH15 9ST, United Kingdom.   (11/93)

QUESTIONNAIRE Standard

Case Title

Case Summary (to be completed by Investigator only)

BUFORA Reference | **Investigator Reference** | **Investigation Complete**

YES   NO   **ON-GOING**

circle

Investigator(s)

Classification
state system used

Primary case date

Primary Location
using OS grid reference where possible

Primary case time
(GMT/BST/LOCAL) using 24 hour clock

Evaluator

Evaluation

SECTION A Biographical Summary

Full name Mr/Mrs/Miss/Ms

Date of birth

Address

Postcode

Telephone number

Recent occupation

Professional, technical or academic qualifications

Special interests/hobbies

Witness signature

Date

The British UFO Research Association is dedicated to the scientific study of the UFO phenomenon.
All BUFORA investigators are bound by a strict Code of Practice which requires them to conduct all
investigations in a professional manner and to respect the anonymity of the witness. A copy of the
Code can be obtained on request from the following address:

BUFORA Ltd, Suite 1, The Leys, 2c Leyton Rd, Harpenden, Hertfordshire, AL5 2TL.

BUFORA Ltd is also registered under the Data Protection Act   Registration Number F0779204

BUFORA Ltd   Registered in London 1234534   Standard Form Issue 2 9/93

SECTION B Written Account
Please write an account of what happened to you

....
....
....
....
....
....
....
....
....
....
....
....
....
....
....

Continue on a separate sheet of paper if required

SECTION C Object Characteristics

Please use this space to sketch what you saw

Please complete the following

Number of objects seen

Colour(s) of object(s) seen

Brightness of object(s) seen
Compared to brightness of full moon

Sound of object(s) seen

Smell of object(s) seen

SECTION D   Object Position

Object altitude

Overhead

Ground level

x

Object direction

N
E
W
S

Imagine yourself at point 'x'. Mark the curved line with an A where you first saw the object and a B where the object was last seen.

Imagine yourself in the middle of the compass dial. Mark the compass with an A where you first saw the object and a B where the object was last seen.

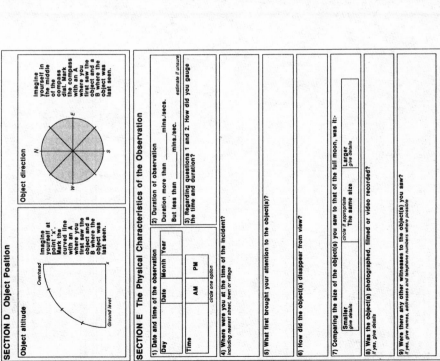

SECTION E   The Physical Characteristics of the Observation

1) Date and time of the observation

Day	Date	Month	Year

Time	AM	PM

circle one option

2) Duration of observation

Duration more than _____ mins./secs.

But less than _____ mins./sec.

estimate if unsure

3) Regarding questions 1 and 2. How did you gauge the time and duration?

4) Where were you at the time of the incident?

including nearest street, town or village

5) What first brought your attention to the object(s)?

6) How did the object(s) disappear from view?

7) Comparing the size of the object(s) you saw to that of the full moon, was it:-

circle if appropriate

Smaller give details	The same size	Larger give details

8) Was the object(s) photographed, filmed or video recorded?

if yes, give details

9) Were there any other witnesses to the object(s) you saw?

if yes, give names, addresses and telephone numbers where possible

SECTION F   Other Characteristics Relating to the Observation

10) Did you, or the surrounding environment, suffer any physical effects which you consider to be attributable to the object(s) seen?

if yes, give details

11) Were you aware of the passage of time around the time of the observation?

if no, describe

12) If you have had any other 'unusual' experiences in your life please describe them

you may feel unable to describe such events; if so, please indicate that there are matters you wish to discuss in a meeting with the investigator

13) Other than the event you have reported, did anything else 'odd' or 'out of place' occur around the time of the observation?

if yes, describe

14) Did any other witnesses experience anything in relation to questions 10, 11, 12 and 13?

if yes, describe

SECTION G   Prevailing Weather during your Observation

	Clear	Hazy	Foggy		
i) Clarity of atmosphere	Clear	Hazy	Foggy		
ii) Cloud cover	None	Quarter	Half	Three Quarter	Total
iii) Atmospheric temperature	Freezing	Cold	Cool	Mild	Warm
iv) Precipitation	Dry	Rain	Snow	Lightning	Other
v) Wind strength	Still	Breeze	Strong Wind	Gale Force	
vi) Visible astronomical objects	Stars	Moon	Sun	Aurora Borealis	Shooting Stars

circle all appropriate responses

Thank you for completing this questionnaire. Now please return it to your local investigator at the address provided. If you require guidance in answering any questions included in this questionnaire, please contact your investigator.

investigator's address

APPENDIX B

The British Ministry of Defence

From: N G Pope, Secretariat(Air Staff)2a, Room 8245

MINISTRY OF DEFENCE
Main Building Whitehall London SW1A 2HB

Telephone | (Direct Dialling) | 071-21-8 2140
| (Switchboard) | 071-21-89000
| (Fax) | 071-21-8

Mr P Mantle
1 Woodhall Drive
Healey Lane
Batley
West Yorks
WF17 7SW

Your reference

Our reference
D/Sec(AS)12/3

Date
25 March 1994

Dear Philip,

Thank you for your letter dated 21 March, in which you asked me to set out our policy and views on the UFO phenomenon.

While the Ministry of Defence does receive some reports of UFO sightings, our only concern is to establish whether or not they pose a threat to the security of the United Kingdom. Unless we judge that they do, and this has not been the case so far, we do not attempt to investigate further, or to identify whatever might have been seen.

It is clear from the reports we receive that there are many strange things to be seen in the sky. However, we believe that explanations could be found for most of them. Possibilities that spring to mind include aircraft lights or aircraft seen from unusual angles, kites, helium balloons, weather balloons, unusual cloud formations, satellites in orbit or satellite debris entering the atmosphere, ball lightning, fireballs and meteorites. We accept, however, that there will always be some sightings that appear to defy explanation, and we are open-minded on these.

Most of the reports we receive relate to little more than vague lights or shapes in the sky. For whatever reason, reports of "close encounters" tend to be made to UFO groups rather than to ourselves. In the absence of any hard evidence, it is not possible to speculate what physical or psychological events might lie behind claims of "close encounters", including abductions. We are not aware of any evidence that would support the existence of extraterrestrial life.

I hope this is helpful, and has explained our position.

Yours sincerely,

Nick Pope

Recycled Paper

Above: The official policy of the British Ministry of defence regarding UFO's.

British Ministry of Defence UFO Sighting Report Form.

REPORT OF AN UNIDENTIFIED FLYING OBJECT

1. Date, time & duration of sighting	
2. Description of object (No of objects, size, shape, colour, brightness, noise)	
3. Exact position of observer (Indoors/outdoors, stationary/moving)	
4. How observed (Naked eye, binoculars, other optical device, camera or camcorder)	
5. Direction in which object first seen (A landmark may be more useful than a roughly estimated bearing)	
6. Angle of sight (Estimated heights are unreliable)	
7. Distance (By reference to a known landmark)	
8. Movements (Changes in 5, 6 & 7 may be of more use than estimates of course and speed)	
9. Met conditions during observations (Moving clouds, haze, mist etc)	
10. Nearby objects (Telephone lines, high voltage lines, reservoir, lake or dam, swamp or marsh, river, high buildings, tall chimneys, steeples, spires, TV or radio masts, airfields, generating plant, factories, pits or other sites with floodlights or night lighting)	

11. To whom reported (Police, military, press etc)	
12. Name & address of informant	
13. Background of informant that may be volunteered	
14. Other witnesses	
15. Date and time of receipt	
16. Any unusual meteorological conditions	
17. Remarks	

Number of UFO sightings reported to the MOD.

1959 – 22	1971 – 379	1983 – 390
1960 – 31	1972 – 201	1984 – 214
1961 – 71	1973 – 233	1985 – 177
1962 – 46	1974 – 177	1986 – 120
1963 – 51	1975 – 208	1987 – 150
1964 – 74	1976 – 200	1988 – 397
1965 – 56	1977 – 435	1989 – 258
1966 – 95	1978 – 750	1990 – 209
1967 – 362	1979 – 550	1991 – 117
1968 – 280	1980 – 350	1992 – 147
1969 – 228	1981 – 600	1993 – 258
1970 – 181	1982 – 250	

Figures from before 1959 are not available.

Geographical distribution of UFO reports from the Ministry Of Defence for the years 1990 to 1993.

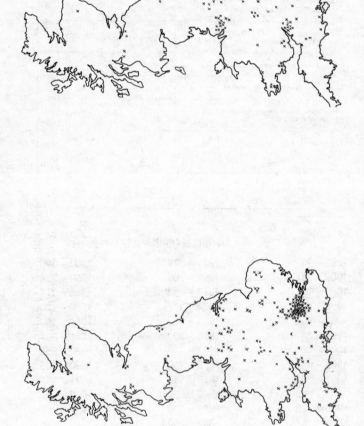

Left: 1990 NB: Concentration of London sightings in January could be due to commercial searchlights bouncing off low cloud also NW London concentration could be caused by rock concert lasers.
Right: 1991

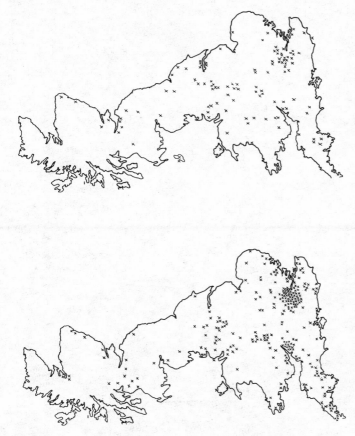

Left: 1992 NB: Concentration of London sightings in mid February due to illuminated airship, also searchlights at music festival in Bristol caused concentration in mid August and in the North some reports of lights in sky were due to what was almost certainly a fireball.

Right: 1993 NB: Waves of London sightings due to airships present over London in March and late November also a fireball on 6th December was reported.

APPENDIX C

The authors would like to hear from anyone who has had similar experiences to those featured in this book. They would also like to hear from anyone who has had a UFO sighting. Complete confidentiality is guaranteed where requested. The authors can be contacted at.

British UFO Research Association,
BM BUFORA,
London,
WC1N 3XX

Recommended UFO research groups:

United Kingdom.

British UFO Research Association, BM BUFORA, London WC1N 3XX.

BUFORA also operates a weekly updated telephone information service. This service regularly reports on all aspects of UFO research from around the world. Available via the British Telecom network you simply have to dial 0891 121886 (calls are 35p per minute off-peak and 45p at all other times).

Contact UK, 11 Ouseley Close, New Marston, Oxford, OX3 OJS.

Manchester UFO Research Association, 6 Silsden Avenue, Lowton, Warrington, Cheshire, WA3 1EN.

Strange Phenomena Investigations, 41 The Braes, Tullibody, Clackmannanshire, Scotland, FK10 2TT.

United States of America

J. Allen Hynek Center for UFO Studies, 2457 West Peterson Avenue, Chicago, Illinois, 60659, USA.

Mutual UFO Network, 103 Oldtowne Road, Seguin, Texas 78155, USA.

Europe

National YFO Center, Jodenstraat 66/102, B-3800 St Truiden, Belgium.

SOS OVNI, BP 324, 13611 Aix-en-Provence, France.

UFO NORWAY, Rygg, N-4448, Gyland, Norway.

Australia

UFO Research Australia, PO Box 229, Prospect, South Australia 5082.

Victorian UFO Research Society, PO Box 43, Moorabbin, Victoria 3189, Australia.

Former Soviet Union.

Research Institute on Anomalous Phenomena, PO Box 4648, Kharkov 310022, Ukraine.

Veronezh UFO Society, Box 1, 394006 Veronezh 6, Russia.